Richard Harris, William Law Murfree

Hints on Advocacy

intended for Practitioners in Civil and Criminal Courts - with suggestions as to

opening a case, examination-in-chief, cross-examination, re-examination, reply,

conduct of a prosecution and of a defense, etc.

Richard Harris, William Law Murfree

Hints on Advocacy
intended for Practitioners in Civil and Criminal Courts - with suggestions as to opening a case, examination-in-chief, cross-examination, re-examination, reply, conduct of a prosecution and of a defense, etc.

ISBN/EAN: 9783337256159

Printed in Europe, USA, Canada, Australia, Japan

Cover: Foto ©Suzi / pixelio.de

More available books at **www.hansebooks.com**

HINTS ON ADVOCACY,

INTENDED FOR PRACTITIONERS

IN CIVIL AND CRIMINAL COURTS,

WITH SUGGESTIONS

AS TO OPENING A CASE, EXAMINATION-IN-CHIEF, CROSS-
EXAMINATION, RE-EXAMINATION, REPLY, CONDUCT
OF A PROSECUTION AND OF A DEFENSE, ETC.,
AND ILLUSTRATIVE CASES;

BY RICHARD HARRIS,

BARRISTER AT LAW, OF THE MIDDLE TEMPLE AND MIDLAND CIRCUIT.

Second American from the Fourth English Edition.

REVISED AND ENLARGED

By WILLIAM L. MURFREE, Sr.

———————

ST. LOUIS, MO.:

WILLIAM H. STEVENSON,

LAW PUBLISHER AND PUBLISHER OF THE
CENTRAL LAW JOURNAL.

1881.

St. Louis, Mo.: Printed by the Central Law Journal.

PREFACE TO THE FIRST ENGLISH EDITION.

THERE is no SCHOOL OF ADVOCACY; there are no LECTURES ON ADVOCACY; and so far as I have been able to ascertain, there is no BOOK on the subject. The young lawyer has to find his way as best he can, very often to the sacrifice of important interests and many unfortunate clients. As he has never learned anything of the *Art of Advocacy*, he is no more fitted for the task of advocating their rights than the clients themselves, except in so far as his knowledge of law will assist him in the purely legal aspects of the question. It seems to me lamentable that no instruction should ever be given in an art which requires an almost infinite amount of knowledge. Tact can not be taught, but it will follow from experience, and a good deal of experience may be condensed into the form of rules. *"I never felt so much in want of a leader as I did when I had to cross-examine that doctor,"* said a talented junior of considerable standing, the other day. Why should this have been? What he had to cross-examine about was simple enough, although the question involved was the sanity or insanity of an individual at a particular time. But he had no rule to guide him, and was simply *adrift*. It is with the hope that some of the observations I have made in the course of my experience may be of some little service to beginners in the profession, and whose want of knowledge of this great practical branch of it is no fault of theirs, that I have ventured to offer them the following "Hints."

TEMPLE, Sept. 17, 1879.

PREFACE TO THE SECOND AMERICAN EDITION.

In revising this admirable work of an English barrister, while discarding matter inapplicable to our system of practice, I have carefully avoided the exclusion of anything of value to the American reader. Seeking to further promote its utility to our young advocates, I have added four new chapters treating respectively of "American Forensic Oratory," "Ethics of Advocacy," "This Honorable Court," and "Gentlemen of the Jury." In Chapter IV. on "Classes of Witnesses," I have ventured to insert sections characterizing the "Expert" witness, the "*Non mi Ricordo*" witness, the "Swift" witness, the "Bullying" witness, and the "Female" witness, as these types appear so frequently on the stand as to entitle them to separate mention.

The success which this little book has achieved has already demonstrated that it supplies a great need, and it is hoped that the changes and additions which have been made will better adapt it to the wants of American students and those young advocates who are still grateful for "Hints."

W. L. MURFREE, Sr.

St. Louis. Mo., April 20, 1881.

TABLE OF CONTENTS.

TABLE OF CONTENTS.

HINTS ON ADVOCACY.

CHAPTER I.— Opening the Case.

It is because I do not know of any book which may be considered as a guide to the aspirant to the honors of the profession (the greatest of which is to be a master of advocacy), that I have taken upon myself to offer the following remarks for his consideration. They are not put forward in a dogmatic spirit, but, on the contrary, with a full consciousness of their imperfections and of their incompleteness when the great subject of which they treat is considered in its vastness and sublimity: but if they should be useful in discovering to the young advocate a dangerous pitfall, or in giving a direction to his unpracticed energies, I shall be pleased that I overcame my scruples as to publishing them.

(1)

SEC. 1. *Common Sense Requisite.*— I shall begin with a proposition, which I do not think will be seriously disputed, namely, that Common Sense is the foundation of good advocacy. A man may be brilliant as an advocate, and even successful, but the mere dazzle of his splendor will be no light to lighten the path of the inexperienced. On the contrary, it may mislead him by its fascinations, and conduct him into dangerous errors. A brilliant advocate may be bold and win by it; or, if he fail, may cover his defeat by masterly and striking efforts, whereas an ordinary person, failing in his attempted imitation, would present but a clumsy appearance in his overthrow. Common sense, invaluable in all human pursuits, is of the utmost importance in advocacy. It is the one quality without which all others are useless, and with which almost all others are superfluous.

Experience smooths the way in all professions; but I have seen so many accidents brought about for want of it, that it may be useful to note some of those principles which seem to guide the leaders of the bar, and which have presented themselves by reason of their constant applicability and usefulness, to my mind, in the form of rules, unwritten, but nevertheless capable of being codified, and certainly deserving of obedience.

I suppose no one will deny that many a good case has been lost by an inexperienced advocate, and many a bad one gained by a skilful one. There is a good deal "in the play," even when you hold an indifferent hand. Anything, therefore, in the shape of a rule which may be useful to a young advocate, either by preventing him from committing a blunder, or assisting him to conduct his case in a fairly creditable manner, must be of some service. An advocate is always dealing with human nature. It is the instrument he works with, and it is the field of his labors. Whether he measures his opponent, or estimates the qualities of the jury, or probes the mind and character of the witness, a knowledge of human nature or human character is the key to success. To treat mankind as mere machines, as some

advocates occasionally do, is to show an utter absence of
that knowledge which is the best acquirement and the first
necessity of an advocate.

§ 2. *How to Treat the Jury.*—The worst thing a man
can do is to treat the jury as though it was composed of so
many fools. Whatever may be their mental capacity,
whether you have a stupid or a wise jury, to treat them as
unworthy your respect is probably to lose your case, and to
discover yourself a man of very little wisdom. There are
almost sure to be one or two shrewd men on the commonest
of common juries; and inasmuch as they will in all probability lead the rest, you must beware of making them your
enemies, as you undoubtedly will, by word or manner, if
you let them suppose that you consider them of little understanding.

A jury is a difficult body to handle, and the more experienced an advocate becomes, the more delicately will he
treat the men who have to decide the fate of his cause.
The persuasive is better than the roaring style, and I have
never known a bawling advocate a successful one in getting
verdicts. A jury invariably endeavors to do what they think
right, and to decide justly : it is inherent in human nature
that they should ; the danger you have frequently to guard
against is, that their very desire to do what is just leads
them at times to an unjust conclusion. They often set up
a rough kind of justice among themselves, and then determine to administer it. The advocate who knows that his
client's rights are opposed to this rude theory of justice
must convince the jury, and bring them, if possible, to a
more legal view. This is not to be accomplished by declamation, but by reason—by combating the notion that has
taken possession of their minds ; it may be an extremely
false or an erroneous one. Before you can succeed in this,
you must ascertain what that idea is, and this you can only
gather by a process of reasoning based upon a knowledge
of human nature. You may or may not touch the right
point ; if you do, and are skilful in your mode of ad-

dress, you will probably overcome it; if you cannot determine what is influencing the jury, so much the worse for your client.   Your knowledge of human nature is at fault, and you may as well sit down.

There is nothing that makes the jury feel more keenly your small appreciation of their mental capacity, than flattering them.   When I say flattering, I mean the coarse and fulsome style exhibited in such expressions as an "intellectual jury," a "jury of freemen," and kindred phrases. There is a flattery that is soothing, pleasing and winning; but to flatter well is an art and gift that. few possess.   It consists in using language which does not itself directly flatter, but leads the hearers to flatter themselves.   It is as subtle and irresistible, as it is charming and delightful.   If you watch a jury while an advocate is telling them that they are something out of the common run of human nature, you will see the same expression on their features that you observe in the faces of the crowd that listens to a peddler while he is praising his wares.   In both cases the hearers know, as well as you do, that you are, to use a common phrase, "humbugging them."   But in the latter case the listeners are amused without being annoyed; in the former, they are generally disgusted, and condemn you as a shallow impostor who would cheat them if you could.   Nothing can be achieved at the bar by artifice, except a contemptible reputation.   But you may accomplish everything by earnestness and an honest employment of those arts without which Genius itself would be but a brilliant failure.

§ 3. *Be Earnest and Logical.*— The most effective way to secure the attention of the jury is to be in earnest, or at least to appear to be.   If you are really so (as you should be), you will communicate something of your own feeling to them.   This is the art of speaking: the carrying your hearers with you in mind and sentiment.

The next thing to observe is to be logical; without this you will not be even intelligible.   Some things you say may be understood, but your address generally will be a jumble of words and a confusion of ideas. I do not by any means imply that you must put both sides logically; by so doing you may reason yourself out of court. It is your own case that I speak of, and it matters little whether you are addressing an educated or an uneducated audience; the mind is a reasoning machine, and it will the more readily grasp arguments that are put logically than those which are presented with unnatural distortions of premiss and sequence.

A skilful and experienced advocate will quickly perceive the master mind of the jury, and to him he will first address himself. Nor will he be long in ascertaining whether he has made an impression or not. If he succeed, he need not trouble himself very much about the rest, unless there are those on the jury who have prejudices against his case. If there are, these prejudices must be attacked, and if possible beaten down; for it will not be sufficient to enlist the *intelligence* of one or two minds against the *prejudices* of others. Intelligence and prejudice are the two master influences on the jury. If there be no prejudice, you wiu by convincing the best mind. If you can not gain the strongest, try to secure the weakest; for if you succeed here, you will not lose your case. The jury are there for you to gain over to your side if you can by fair and legal argument, by presenting your case agreeably to their minds and sentiments. I do not say you ought to appeal to the passions or sympathies of a jury, but it is perfectly allowable to leave the jury to make that appeal for themselves. The man who would directly solicit compassion is a poor advocate, but he who would present the facts of his case so that the jury may regard his client with that sentiment is a great one. The one knows human nature, the other does not. The one awakens your sympathy, the other rouses your contempt.

§ 4. *Fine Talking.*—One great evil to avoid if you would be understood and appreciated, either by a common jury or a special, is fine talking. Fine language will not stand the wear and tear of an ordinary *nisi prius* contest, and nowhere (except, perhaps, in the ears of a romantic female).

is it so powerful and effective as good well-chosen homely words. It is as unnatural as the spangled dress of the acrobat, and as utterly unfitted for the ordinary business of a work-a-day life. One has often seen advocates mystify their meaning in phrases which were more like a girlish novelist's hysterical utterances, than the sound language of a man and a scholar. It will take a good and gifted speaker a long time, and will require a great deal of practice, before he can venture to embellish his address with the figures or the fancies of rhetoric; indeed, the most gifted and the most finished speaker will only use them in a limited manner; profuseness of ornamentation, like a redundancy of words, being at all times more calculated to obscure the meaning than to elucidate it; and above all things affectation should be avoided. Every listener detests it, and cannot help feeling some degree of contempt for the person who indulges in it. Affectation is a weakness even with strong minds, and although it is sometimes tolerated in a clever man, it is never admired; when an ordinary individual indulges in it, he is simply despised.

A quiet style is always more powerful than a noisy one. I have never seen a verdict obtained by noise; foam has no weight, fury of language no force. I by no means say that a conversational style is powerful; on the contrary, you might just as well attempt to set fire to a bed of growing bulrushes with a piece of tinder, as to rouse a jury by a feeble speech.

But at the bar, except in rare cases, the higher gifts of oratory are out of place. It is a limited field; it has its beaten tracks, and along these men must travel. Oratory is not one of its paths; in other words, attempts at what is commonly called oratory are to be avoided. What a figure an advocate would present, who should attempt the flights of Burke or Sheridan in a "running down" case! What is really required is a well-told simple narrative of the facts in opening your case to the jury. The fewer the words, the better; and the less argument, the more likely is your statement to be believed. It must seem a strange story to the jury that requires arguing upon before the other side have had a syllable to say in contradiction.

§ 5. *Arguing too Soon.*—An advocate will sometimes tell the jury in his opening that the plaintiff was on his proper side of the way, and that he will convince them that that must have been so, because, etc., etc. This is as bad as an opening can be, because it casts a doubt at the very commencement upon the truth of his own story. The best reason for the jury's believing your story before contradiction is that your witnesses swear to it. When the other side have brought facts or arguments in conflict with it, your time of argument will have arrived, and your arguments will have a freshness which, if used before, they would not possess ; they will work as if their edge had not been taken off by a clumsy use of them when there was nothing to cut. When there is no grist, the miller stops his mill.

Another advantage from not arguing too soon will be that your adversary will not be able to turn your arguments against yourself, or to fit his own in accordance with your theories. In other words, you had better obtain some knowledge of your opponent's hand before throwing away your best cards.

At the expense of repetition I have endeavored to impress this point upon the student's attention, because it seems to me of the greatest importance ; a good case may be thrown away by a weak and indiscreet opening.

§ 6. *Show Your Belief in Your Case.*—The first thing to be done in opening a case is to impress the jury with the idea that at least you believe in it yourself. This may seem almost too obvious a truism to mention, and no doubt it is present to the mind of every advocate. We all know it, or believe we do. The student himself will say, "Of course you must make the jury believe that you think your case is an honest one. Everybody knows that." Granted ; but it is not the knowing it that I am inculcating, but a very different thing, viz., the making the jury believe this. I have seen advocates whose manner was such that they scarcely ever seemed to believe in their own case. A want of seriousness characterized their tone and language. This is a fatal blunder of style. There is nothing which a jury so much detests in the person addressing them as an air of jaunty frivolity. One need hardly say that this is quite a distinguishable quality from humor, for which it is often intended. Humor, when it can be introduced with propriety, is one of the most insinuating of qualities; is almost always acceptable, and is one of the most fascinating as well as successful of an advocate's gifts. But you must have the genuine article and not the spurious imitation, between which there is as much difference as between a hearty laugh and the grin of a dog that runs about through the city. There is another evil—not the least under the sun in advocacy—which consists in constantly anticipating your opponent's case. It is a similar fault to that of arguing in defense of your assertions before they are attacked, but a trifle perhaps more dangerous. Some advocates think it proper to anticipate the defense and attempt to demolish it. The law now-a-days does not permit it; he has the right to present his case, and it will be your duty, if you can, to demolish it afterwards. Even if you know the exact line he is going to take, it is not always advisable to meet him half-way. But in ninety-nine cases out of a hundred you do not know the manner in which his case will be presented, although you may know what his defense is. After he has placed it before you and employed his arguments, you know the exact line he has taken; and if you cannot beat him then, it is quite certain you could not have done so before. Do not spring at your adversary before he is over the ditch, otherwise you may find yourself uncomfortably landed in the middle.

One often hears a youthful (and sometimes a not youthful) advocate say, " he cannot conceive what defense his learned friend can have"—that "it is really, gentlemen, an undefended case." And yet, very often these remarks

are followed, more often than not, with a verdict for the
learned friend who has no case or no defense. It is impossible to conceive of anything more ineffective than this.
Such assertions are worse than useless. They are no part
of the opening; they are not argument; they lend no emphasis to the statement; and they are not true. They impress neither judge nor jury; but they sometimes make the
counsel who utters them look extremely ridiculous. If the
learned gentleman on the other side has no case, it will appear without your saying so. If he has a case, your saying
he has none will not alter the fact. This is nothing more
than an old, worn-out "dodge" of an almost extinct school
of advocacy. It is a selfish assumption and an overbearing
piece of arrogance on the part of the advocate employing
it, as though he would not only proclaim himself the judge
and jury in his own cause, but even deprive his opponent of
the right of being heard in his defense.

§ 7. *Redundancy and Illustration.*—It would be out of
place perhaps to say anything further with regard to redundancy of expression, were it not a prominent fault with many
young advocates. It is a pleasant thing, no doubt, to air
one's eloquence in public, but it reminds one of the process
of airing other articles—it shows a good many weak places.
The fewest words, as a rule, make the best speech. All
the language not required to convey ideas is surplusage,
and if used at all, should be of the very best; if not required for use, it should be employed for the purpose of
lending dignity or moderate embellishment. It may be said
that baldness of expression is not compatible with excellence. That may be true, and I am not unaware that the
graces of eloquence lend a charm to the speaker as well as
the speech. These, doubtless, should be cultivated and employed when in a state of cultivation, but not before.
Redundancy, however, is not a grace, but a deformity, and
the way to cultivate that is to cut it off altogether. Poverty of language is one thing, choice of words another, and
be the greatest poverty of language with the

greatest redundancy of words. One has often heard speakers talk for half-an-hour without making a single sentence, reminding one of a muddy rivulet after a deluge, winding its way wherever it can find an outlet or an inlet, making a great fuss, and never coming to a single stop or a conclusion. Of course, no one would say that ornamentation is to be ignored. On the contrary, it should be carefully used, but not so as to smother that which it should render more attractive.

Illustration, sparingly employed, is an effective ornament; and so much so, that there is often a danger of even truth and reason being sacrificed to it. Minds are apt to be carried away by a beautiful simile, and because that is true, are prone to consider that the argument illustrated must be true also. But in an opening speech, illustration should be utterly abandoned. Fact, and fact alone, is the strength of an opening speech; although when I come to deal with the examples further on, I will endeavor to point out how the facts may be commented upon, when necessary, by way of explanation, connection or emphasis.

§ 8. *Arrangement and Order.*—The principal thing in an opening speech is *arrangement and order*. No really good statement can be made without this; and time will never be wasted in noting up and arranging a case so as to present it chronologically to the jury.

It may be said no one doubts that order and arrangement are necessary to make a good opening statement. It is so true, that every one knows it and no one denies it; but so long as so many advocates act as if they did not know it, and neglect not only all order, method and arrangement, but confuse facts and dates to the annoyance of jury and judge and to the disparagement of their client, it seems not unnecessary to insist that the strictest attention should be paid to the order of time, the order of facts, and the arrangement of causes and effects. Every statement should be as free from confusion, as if the facts had been mapped out on paper with the utmost faithfulness. Every series of facts should be brought down in the strictest order; and if there be many series operating apart, but exercising an influence upon the main action of the drama, they should be brought down in their natural order and sequence until they are all centered upon the common point. In the most complicated and tangled circumstances there should be no confusion. It is the business of the advocate and the art of advocacy to separate them, and to show their relations to one another, their bearing upon each other, and their influence upon the main action. Irrelevant matter, therefore, should be carefully excluded—by no means so easy a task as it at first sight appears, and only to be accomplished by diligent study and thoughtful practice.

What is understood by irrelevant matter, is matter which attaches itself to or mixes itself up with the circumstances of the case without any natural connection with or bearing upon the case itself. There are always facts which, in one sense, may be said to be irrelevant, but which in reality are not so. And examples might be given in cases of actions for malicious prosecution, where events or conversations that operated upon the mind of the prosecutor have to be considered. So in cases of libel; and so, in fact, in most inquiries where the state of mind of an individual is either the main subject of inquiry or has to be considered.

What is the *issue*, and *upon what evidence will it depend?* Determine that first, and then the evidence will arrange itself almost naturally. But in many cases, that which should be first settled in the advocate's mind is never distinctly perceived.

As an instance, take the following pleadings :— A endeavors to set up a lost will. He alleges that it was made and executed on a certain day five years ago, and that it never was revoked. The defendant denies the making in accordance with the requirements of the statute. He says that the alleged testator was not of sound mind, memory and understanding ; that the will was afterwards destroyed while he was of sound mind, memory and understanding, with the intention of revoking it, and that the plaintiff is not a legatee. Now it will be obvious here that many issues will present themselves ; but it may be equally apparent to the counsel for the plaintiff that the whole question may ultimately resolve itself into this, whether some particular witness saw the will at a particular time. This will perhaps depend not upon the accuracy of the witness' memory, but upon his credibility. The decision, therefore, may depend entirely upon the question as to whether a witness can be believed or not. The execution may be past all question ; the sanity of the testator indisputable upon the evidence ; the contents provable by some draft or otherwise ; the question of destruction or no by the testator, up to a given moment, uncontroverted ; the insanity of the testator from a given time also placed beyond doubt ; the issue, therefore, will resolve itself into the question whether the will was in existence between two given periods, and that must depend upon the evidence to this fact of the person who saw it in the meantime. If he be believed, verdict for the plaintiff ; if disbelieved, for the defendant.

Now, it will be obvious that to lay much stress upon those points which will be placed beyond all dispute as the evidence is unfolded would be wasted energy. The facts should of course be stated with due precision and conciseness, but to dwell upon them would only be wearying the jury to no purpose, and diverting their attention from the proper object of inquiry. The thing really to be done is to impress them with the reliability of your witness ; if they disbelieve him, your case is lost ; therefore you must guard him against the assaults of your opponent, whose skill will be directed to breaking him down. He will know that this is the key of your position. But how is the witness to be strengthened? If you have no corroboration, must he not stand by himself? By no means. A hundred incidents in the story to which your witness speaks may be corroborated by other testimony, and this will tend to show his truthfulness. You must search for this kind of corroboration when you have no other, and if you find that he is generally supported by other and, it may be, totally independent witnesses, upon points which neither he nor they deemed material ; if you find that the story is consistent in itself, and is likewise compatible with the probabilities of the case, you may rely upon it that the verdict will be yours.

It might not be out of place here, to mention that this will show the absolute necessity of a careful examination-in-chief. If that has been clumsy and disconnected, if only half the story has been told, the very probabilities I have been speaking of will become improbabilities, and your witness will not only be unsupported but weakened. It will be seen also from this illustration, how important a part reason exercises in matters of this kind. The jury will neither believe nor disbelieve a witness without a reason satisfactory to their own minds. You must, therefore, take care that every fact upon which a fair argument in favor of your theory can be based is not only elicited in examination-in-chief, but stored up in your memory, to be reproduced to the jury for the purpose of influencing their judgment.

§ 9. *Making an Impression.*— And here, it may be observed, there is a mode of creating an impression on the mind of a jury without in the least appearing to desire it, and which is of all others the most effective. All men are more or less vain, and every man gives himself credit for a deal of discernment. He loves to find out things for himself—to guess the answer to a riddle better than to be told it—to think he can see as far into an opaque substance as most people. In many instances jurymen will see farther into a case than either judge or counsel, and will sometimes correctly decide upon a cause for some reason that is not apparent and is never ascertained. The most experienced counsel is often puzzled at a verdict, the reasons for which are sound and good, and yet which arose from no effort on his part or that of his opponent, but simply out of a common-sense view of the facts as they presented themselves to the unprofessional mind. If you want a point thoroughly to impress the jury, do not actually make it, if you can effect your object by a less direct means ; let the jury make it for themselves, only be sure that it is made. You may be too venturesome and too clever, which is a great deal worse than not being clever enough.

Mystery is an excellent wrapper for an important fact, especially when you let the jury undo it for themselves. Say that a will mysteriously disappears between two given times. If your case is that A. B., who took no share under it, and who would be benefited by its destruction, in all probability took the will away, you need go no further than state that there is no evidence as to the disappearance of the instrument ; that the niece who was interested in its preservation and the doctor were the only persons who were in the house between those times. If then you show that A. B., for ever so brief a moment, came to the house, the jury will as a matter of course come to the conclusion in their own minds, without any direct charge on your part, that A. B. destroyed it, and upon very slight evidence indeed give a verdict in favor of the non-destruction of the will by the testator. The jury in fact will draw all necessary inferences for themselves.

This is not a mere " trick " of advocacy ; if it were, it would be better not to mention it. Tricks are the resources of feeble advocates, and the worst or the best feature of a trick is that it always fails in its object. It is known instantly, and damages the cause it is intended to serve, as the advertisements of a quack doctor proclaim his imposture.

§ 10. *Tricks.*— What is the use of endeavoring to prejudice the cause of your opponent by saying : " Gentlemen, I don't say that the defendant has obtained these goods by false pretenses, but I say his mode of dealing will not commend itself to your minds." This is a trick—an impoverished one, it is true ; but so would every other one seem if I were to write it down. Look at the following : " I don't think much of such and such a transaction ; I merely call

your attention to it in passing; or the fact that the defendant did or said so and so.'' These are devices which do not
approach to the pretensions of art, and are unworthy of a
good speaker. They are not the truth—not the words of
sincerity; and when you have neither truth nor sincerity,
although you may have acting, you cannot have the highest
and best speaking. Truth and sincerity are among the
charms and graces of eloquence, and they are the power that
stirs and impresses an audience. I am far from saying that
there are not two ways of presenting a sound proposition or
an incontrovertible argument. Truth and sincerity themselves may, in an uncultured and inartistic speaker, be made
to look absolutely offensive, and not only to look so, but to
be so. Therefore it is absolutely necessary, if you would
impress your hearers, that art should come to the aid of
reason; the same idea and the same truth may be conveyed
in coarse as well as in cultured language. One need not say
in which it will be transmitted most effectively; but the
tricks referred to are·apart from both, and partake more of
the style appropriate to the conjuror or wizard at a fair than
to an advocate speaking at the bar.

Tricks of expression are nearly allied to tricks of gesture
and facial distortions, such as one laments to observe occasionally even in these refined and polished times. Some advocates twist their faces into a look of extreme anguish when
they address a jury, as though the weight of their task
caused them physical torture. Others attempt to screw
their features into looks of supreme contempt, anger, or
scorn. Every one will acknowledge this to be altogether
bad. The face takes its expression from the feelings; and
you can no more give it a natural look which does not spring
from that natural source than you could make the face of an
india-rubber doll beam with pleasure. It is only by dint of
labor and study that the sculptor can obtain an expression
upon the marble which faintly represents the emotions. It
is quite clear every one is not artist enough to put the right
muscles in motion to produce a corresponding effect upon

his own features whenever he desires it.   Attempts of this kind are not only ludicrous but foolish.   I have seen an advocate, in trying to look angry, cause a titter all round the court, and set the jury on the grin.   He was attempting a piece of acting, and not being an actor, failed.   He pulled the wrong muscles of his face, if I may be permitted the expression.   A photographer is often blamed for not producing a "good likeness," when the fault is with the sitter, who either attempts to look learned, or interesting, or heroic, or anything, in short, but what he is.   Do you suppose every one could put his face in a hole in the canvas, and look a good likeness of himself?   I think not.   Men are such poor actors as a rule, that they cannot even " look themselves" if they try to.   I have seen another shake his head very much, and stoop to the jury in a mode which must have suggested to Dickens the " jury droop," and turn up his eyes to watch the effect; this was intended for pathos.   It did not answer; a bad actor and a grinning audience was all it came to.

All acting that shows itself to be acting is bad, and at the bar perhaps is more out of place than anywhere else.   The instant the jury suspect you of attempting to deceive them, their confidence in you will be gone, and they will pay no attention to any argument you may use.   They will suspect the most sound and plausible as being only the more deceitful.   If you feel in earnest—as you should whatever your cause—your features will exhibit all the emotions they are intended by nature to display without any effort or contrivance on your part.   And this you may be sure of, that if you do not attempt any facial display, you will never pull the wrong muscles.

§ 11. *Imitation.*—It is perhaps as well here to warn the young advocate against a very common and fascinating error— that of imitation.   A really good advocate has a style of his own, and an individuality which would be utterly spoilt, were he to attempt to blend it with that of another.   To imitate a successful man's style is like a short man put ting on a tall man's coat. However well it fitted the one, it is sure to look ridiculous on the other. Style is born with a man as much as his mental capacity itself. Nor should it be forgotten that imitators, as a rule, adopt the failings and not the excellencies of their models. Affectations of speech and mannerisms are what generally catch the eye of the imitator. Besides this, imitations are bad in themselves. As a rule they are grotesque, and frequently little more than burlesques of the original. It is at once apparent that they are no part of the imitator's individuality, however well they may be done.

It does not of course follow that the best advocates are not therefore to be accurately studied. On the contrary, it is servile imitation that is to be deprecated, and not the careful study of the graces and excellencies of the best men. The smooth, unruffled demeanor, the courtesy, the polished ease, the unexaggerated eloquence, the order and arrangement of speeches, the skilful and subtle modes of cross-examination, the fearless independence of the masters of advocacy, should be studiously considered. Imitate these—if you can. But wherever you see an extravagance of style, even though it may be fascinating in the advocate to whom it is natural, never be tempted for a moment to imitate that. An imitator must of necessity be a second or third-rate man, and is generally below even that.

§ 12. *Arrangement of Facts.*—To open a strong case is not to prove it. What you should strive to do is to give the substance (somewhat more than an outline) of the case you intend to prove. This should be done so that when the evidence, usually in disjointed and often in widely-separated pieces, is presented piece by piece to the jury, they may see the bearings of each upon that which has gone before and afterwards upon the whole, and appreciate its value.

Suppose you have a number of witnesses to prove various facts, totally separate and apparently disconnected from one another, but yet having a bearing directly or indirectly upon the main issue. These witnesses represent numerous facts,

18 HINTS ON ADVOCACY.

distinct and separate, occurring at different times and in different places, yet all working towards a common center, confirming and corroborating one another, leading up to and indeed forcing on the main event of the story. It is obvious that in opening a case of this kind, if you would make the narrative clear, you must deal completely with one set of facts at a time—the earliest in date will probably be the best to commence with. These should be made plain and intelligible to the jury merely as facts, and no attempt should be made to show their bearing upon the main point of the case until the other branches of the subject are in like manner made intelligible. If this be done too early, the effect will be lost, the narrative will be disturbed, and the minds of the hearers confused. The first set of facts should be stated and left ready to be fitted in at the right time. The next, and the next will follow in proper order, until at last the whole of your materials will be ready to be built up into the structure you intend to form.

The jury having thus seen the separate parts of your narrative, will perceive readily what position each will occupy, and what relation it will bear to the others.

It need scarcely be said that if you make any part out of due proportion to the rest by exaggeration, it will not fit in, and will spoil the symmetry of the whole ; nor should the statement be flimsily adorned with superfluous eloquence, as they dress out an animal with tawdry ribbons when the creature is about to be baited ; nor overlaid with prejudice, which is equally unnecessary in a good case or a bad one. No advocate need attempt to infuse prejudice, but on the contrary should be on his guard to prevent its influence. You should seek only to make your statement appear truthful and natural. Short of this, the opening will be a failure ; beyond this, the evidence will be.

§ 13. *Moderation.* — " Your opening," said a distinguished Queen's Counsel to his opponent, "was admirable ; it combined moderation with such wonderful force." The moderation, in fact, was its force. It was a case in which

there was a multitude of facts, and various sets of them ;
but in which, if two facts were true, the whole must be, because the relations of these two to the remainder were such
that the fabric could not exist without them, and must exist
in its entirety if those facts occupied the respective positions
assigned to them.   While speaking of moderation, it may
be as well to say that it is equally necessary to moderate
the tone as the style.   It enables a speaker the better to exhibit the most beautiful of all the graces of eloquence,
namely, that of modulation.   This is the music of speaking, little cultivated I fear at the bar, or anywhere else except the stage, but one which is of inestimable value in
forensic speaking, and one that ought to be practiced with
the utmost diligence.   There are some few orators still liv-
ing, who possess this charm in perfection.

§ 14. *Soft Speaking a Fault.*— There is another fault
which is equally well to guard against as loud speaking,
and that is soft speaking.   Speak out ! don't mumble and
drawl out your words as though they were tape you were
selling by the yard, and were not certain how much you had
in stock.   A man who bellows may get on at the bar to a
certain extent, but if you are afflicted with an inaudible
voice you will not get on at all.   One does not like to see
the expression of pain on a juryman's face as, with his
hand behind his ear and his mouth open (as though he
might catch something in that way), he is straining to hear
what the advocate is talking about.   Sometimes diffidence
produces softness of speech ; if so, perseverance will overcome it ; but it is doubtful if the diffident young advocate
will have much opportunity for perseverance in court.   But
there are places where he may persevere as much as he
likes.   There are seashores and windy commons.

But the most trying, and by no means the least useful of
places for practice, is the quiet room.   To speak to one's
self requires some energy and a considerable amount of
courage.   You have to surmount the idea of the foolishness
of the situation, and it constantly presses upon you ; you

have to listen to the tones of your own voice, and these, unless you stand excessively high in your own opinion, sound like self-reproaches; you are sometimes carried away by wild flights of extravagant oratory, like one going up in a balloon; and then it suddenly collapses; and as you come down, you cannot for the life of you help thinking what an eccentric person you are. But it is because of all these thoughts and feelings arising out of the absurdity of the situation, and the grotesqueness of the fact of a man's declaiming to himself, that the exercise is so useful; and if one can conquer his diffidence in his own room, he will be sure to master it in public. Besides this, the being able to listen to and criticize one's own words will be of immense benefit; and if he have any power at all of modulating the voice, he will be able to exercise it here, where no other sound interposes. It is here, if anywhere, he will be able to tune it and to test its capabilities.

There is, doubtless, too little attention paid to this branch of advocacy. A good many proceed as if men were universally gifted with a fine flexible voice, with sweet eloquence, and the art of using both to perfection. Whereas, the gift of a rich voice is one of the rarest, and requires cultivation before it can be rendered perfect. How much more is it necessary to tune those voices that are not rich and very often are not even pleasant?

§ 15. *Rapidity a Fault.*— It may not be superfluous, in concluding this chapter, to say that a speaker, in opening a case, should never be rapid. As a rule, rapidity of utterance is not a common fault, but there are many who talk too fast, and as a necessary consequence say too little. It is difficult for all who are not the most finished speakers to make a sentence, and it is not easy for juries to follow at times deliberate speakers who can form sentences; but what must their difficulty be in following a man who speaks with great volubility, and never makes a sentence at all? "Can't make head or tail of him," said a juror, after a flippant junior had sat down, "talks too fast." "What's the action for?" asked another. " Is he for pla-antive or defendant?" inquired a third. An advocate had better not open his case at all, if he cannot leave a better impression than this—he is simply injuring his client.

Slow, sure and short, is a good motto for young advocates. A long opening is wearisome and unnecessary, and it can only be made more so by repetition. Not that you can deal out speeches by the yard, and cut them off in lengths as required. I am speaking with reference to verbiage rather than time. A speech may be very long that occupies twenty minutes : it may be admirably concise and take six hours in its delivery. The opening in the Tichborne trial for perjury occupied some days, yet it is a model of neatness, arrangement, and concise narrative.

A short speech is more powerful than a long one, and when jurymen tap the ledge of their desk with impatient fingers, you may take it for granted you have been already too long, and every additional word may be not only a burden to them. but also to your client. Consistently, therefore, with those graces of diction without which language would sometimes be offensively bald, the fewer words you employ, the better. It by no means follows that you should speak in telegrams, but that mere verbiage should be pruned away, so that there may be greater strength and a more symmetrical and cultured beauty. The jury care little for the advocate's conceits ; they want the facts of the case, and it is precisely because they require these only, that you must present them in a form that will not only impress them upon their memory, but induce an acceptance of them in accordance with your view and your client's interest.

§ 16. *Spurious Pathos.*— Another error to avoid is that of attempting pathos ; it is almost sure to make the jury laugh. A weeping advocate and a laughing audience is a scene for farce, and not for a court of justice. The power of moving the passions is the highest and rarest gift that nature bestows on an orator. It is so great that it may be called oratory itself. But this mastery over the feelings does not come by practice ; it cannot be acquired, nor is a speaker pathetic by choice. He may weep, if he be weak enough, but that is not pathos ; he may shake his head, hold up his hands, do anything else to mimic feeling, but he will not move his audience. Fortunately it is a gift little needed at the bar ; on the contrary, if one be endowed with it, it will be his duty to suppress rather than to encourage it. To attempt an appeal to the passions without possessing the power, is but to declare yourself an impostor, and to show that you would act unfairly if you could. There may be occasions when an advocate's cause appeals to the deepest feelings of our nature. Those are times when, if you have the power, you may use it legitimately and even nobly in behalf of the oppressed or the injured ; but if you have not the high gift, you had better not spoil the pathos of facts by a ridiculous burlesque of sublime sentiment.

In conclusion, it may be remarked that men who have attained eminence as speakers have reached it only by immense labor, by unwearied practice, and by a dilligent study of the greatest masters. It may seem superfluous to go through so severe a training merely to become a *Nisi Prius* advocate ; but when one considers that to speak well is almost to ensure success, it must be conceded I think, that success is worth all the labor of our lives to achieve. And further it must not be forgotten that the time may come when some great occasion will demand, whether at the bar or elsewhere, the latent powers which have been stored up by the earnest labors of one's early years.

CHAPTER II.—The Examination in Chief.

One of the most important branches of advocacy is the examination of a witness in chief. As a rule, a young lawyer, if he be bold, and he may be bold through fear, throws himself into his work like one who plunges into the water before he can swim. There must, under such circumstances, be much floundering and confusion. The nervousness that is necessarily felt when he rises in court before an experienced judge, whose eye is like a microscope for his faults, and who is not always tender in his criticism, would be a terrible drawback, even if the junior were master of his work. As a rule, however, he has very little notion as to how a witness should be examined. He feels, too, that there are around him those who are too prone to "mark what is done amiss," not from ill-nature, by any means, but from habit. His nervousness increases in proportion as his want of practical experience makes itself more and more manifest to himself.   One can scarcely conceive of a situation more unenviable than this.   I do not pretend that any observations about to be made will cure all this, or give him experience; but it is hoped that some of my remarks will so far be advantageous as to enable him to avoid many errors, and to keep in the well-trodden path of experienced advocates.

§ 17. *The Position of a Witness.*—One fact should be remembered to start with, and it is this : The witness whom he has to examine has probably a plain straightforward story to tell, and upon the telling it depends the belief or disbelief of the jury, and their consequent verdict.   If it were to be told amid a social circle of friends, it would be narrated with more or less circumlocution and considerable exactness.   But all the facts would come out; and that is the first thing to insure if the case be, as I must all along assume it to be, an honest one.   I have often known half a story told, and that the worse half too, the rest having to be got out by the leader in re-examination, if he have the opportunity.   If the story were being told as I have suggested, in private, all the company would understand it, and if the narrator were known as a man of truth, all would believe him.   It would require no advocate to elicit the facts or to confuse the dates; the events would flow pretty much in their natural order.   Now change the audience; let the same man attempt to tell the same story in a court of justice.   His first feeling is that he must not tell it in his own way.   He is going to be examined upon it; he is to have it dragged out of him piece-meal, disjointedly, by a series of questions—in fact, he is to be interrupted at every point in a worse manner than if everybody in the room, one after another, had questioned him about what he was going to tell, instead of waiting till he had told it.   It is not unlike a *post mortem;* only the witness is alive, which seems almost a misfortune to him.   He knows, too, that every word he says will probably be disputed, if not flatly contradicted. He has never had his word disputed before perhaps, but now it is very likely to be suggested that he is committing rank perjury.

This is pretty nearly the state of mind of many a witness, when for the first time he enters the box to be examined. In the first place then, he is in the worst possible frame of mind to be examined—he is agitated, confused, and bewildered. Now put, to examine him, an agitated, confused and bewildered young advocate, and you have got the worst of all elements together for the production of what is wanted, namely, evidence. First of all the man is asked his name, as if he were going to say his catechism, and much confusion there is often about that, the witness feeling sometimes that he is blamed by the judge for not having a more agreeable one, or for having a name at all. He looks, however, as if he could not by any possibility have helped it, and thinks he has got off remarkably well so far. Then he faces the young counsel, and wonders what will be the next question.

§ 18. *Let him Tell his own Story in his own Way.*— Now the best thing the advocate can do under these circumstances is to remember that the witness has something to tell, and that but for him, the advocate, he would probably tell it very well, "in his own way." *The fewer interruptions therefore, the better;* and *the fewer questions, the less questions will be needed.* Watching should be the chief work; especially to see that the story be not confused with extraneous and irrelevant matter. The chief error the witness will be likely to fall into will be hearsay evidence, either he says to somebody, or somebody says to him something which is inadmissible and delays the progress of events. But the witness being very tender, you must be very careful how you check the progress of his " he says, says he's," or you may turn off the stream altogether.

§ 19. *Form of Questions.*— The most useful questions for eliciting facts are the most commonplace. "What took place next?" being infinitely better than putting a question from the narrative in your brief, which leads the witness to

contradict you. The interrogative "Yes?" as it asks nothing and yet everything, is better than a rigmarole phrase,
such as, "Do you remember what the defendant did or said
upon that?" The witness, after such a question, generally
feels puzzled, as if you were asking him a conundrum which
is to be passed on to the next person after he has given it
up.

Judges frequently rebuke juniors for putting a question
in this form: "Do you remember the 29th of February
last?" In the first place, it is not the *day* that has to be
remembered at all, and whether the witness recollects it or
not, is immaterial. It is generally the *facts* that took place
about that time you want deposed to, and if that date is at
all material, you are putting the question in the worst possible form to get it. A witness so interrogated begins to
wonder whether he remembers the day, or whether he does
not, and becomes puzzled. You might just as well ask if he
remembers the 1st day of May, 1816 (the day on which he
was born), instead of asking him the date of his birth.
This is one of the commonest, and at the same time one of
the stupidest blunders that can be made. I will, therefore,
at the risk of repetition, give one more illustration.
Suppose you ask a witness if he remembers the 10th of
June, 1874; he probably does not, and both he and you
are bewildered, and think you are at cross purposes; but
ask him if he was at Niagara in that year, and you will get
the answer without hesitation; inquire when it was, and he
will tell you the 10th of June. In this way you avoid tax-
ing a witness's memory; always a dangerous proceeding,
and much more within the province of cross-examination
than examination-in-chief. Many a good case has been
lost, and many more will be, by clumsy questions of this
kind at the commencement of a witness's examination.
If you leave his mind in a state of bewilderment and confusion, your work will only need to be followed up by a well
delivered question or two in cross-examination, to demolish
the whole of his evidence; and then, in all probability, the

advocate will think he would certainly have won if he had not had so stupid a witness.

§ 20. *To Examine Well a Difficult Task.*—Incalculable mischief is done by a clumsy examination, and yet as little attention is paid to this branch of advocacy as to any. Everyone thinks it is so easy, that a blunder is impossible. I believe it to be the most difficult task of all—it certainly is the most important; because your evidence is your case. It may seem unnecessary to observe that no sign of irritability should be manifested toward the witness. If he be stupid, your vexation will by no means assist him, nor will a sharp rebuke, such as one too often hears administered. The more stupid he, the more patient should the advocate be. Every question should not only be intelligible and relevant in itself, but it should be put in such a form that its relevancy to the case may be apparent to him. A question, without being leading, should be a reminder of events rather than a test of the witness's recollection. I will give an illustration which will show how easy it is to blunder, and how necessary it is to avoid blundering.

§ 21. *Illustration of how Not to Examine.*—A man brings an action against a railway company for false imprisonment. The facts are these: He lost his ticket and refused to pay; the porter on the platform called the inspector, who sent for a policeman and then gave him into custody. The best way not to get the facts out is to examine him in the following manner:—

" Were you asked for your ticket?—Yes."

" Did you produce it?—No."

" Why not?—I had lost it."

" Are you sure you took it?—Quite."

" Positive? (This is a good opening, surely, for the thin edge of the wedge of cross-examination — a doubt thrown on your own witness).—I am quite sure."

" What did the defendant say then; I mean the porter? " (This blunder ought not to have been made.) At this

point the witness is in a hopeless muddle, and says; " I
was given into custody."

The story is not half told, although it is one of the simplest to tell.

Now the counsel contradicts by way of explanation, and
says " No, no ; do attend." Witness strokes his chin as
though about to be shaved. Judge glances at him, and wonders if he's lying. Counsel for the defendants (sure to be
eminent) smile, and the jury look knowingly at one another, and begin to think it's a trumped-up attorney's action.

Now start again with another question.

" When the train stopped you got out?—I didn't get out
afore it stopped, sir."

" Did any one ask you for your ticket?—They did ;"
emphatically, as though he knows now where he is.

"Who?—I'm sure I don't know who he is ; never see the
man before in my life."

" Well, well, did he do anything?—No, sir, he didn't do
nothin' as I knows of ;" evidently puzzled, as if he had forgotten some important event upon which the whole case
turns.

This looks so ridiculous on paper that it is possible some
readers will doubt if it ever happened. I can only say
there are many much more ridiculous incidents that occur
in courts of justice when young counsel have what is called
a " stupid " witness in the box. In court the stupidity
always seems to be that of the witness. On paper it looks
as if the learned counsel could establish a better title to it.
This leads me to notice a cardinal rule in examination-in-
chief. It is seldom regarded as such by beginners, and
only seems to be observed as the result of experience. Why
it should not be learnt at once and implicitly obeyed, I do
not know, except it be that it has never been written down.

§ 22. *Order of Time should be Observed.*—The rule I refer to is, that in examining a witness the order of time

ought always to be observed. Stated in writing it looks simple enough, and everybody says " of course." Plain as one of the ten commandments, and as often violated by young advocates. Just step into court, and you will see events running over one another like ants on an ant hill. Not only is the rule not acted upon, it is never even considered. True, the principal events in a story are generally placed in something like order, because the judge requires that his notes should be correct. But with what difficulty this is accomplished when an inexperienced junior gets out a detail here and a detail there and mixes them up with wrong events and dates, leaving the judge to match them as if he were playing a game of " Patience !"

While a witness is telling his story in a natural manner (which he will generally do if left to himself) and with due attention to the order of time, counsel suddenly breaks in with some such observation as this : " One moment. What was said when you spoke to the defendant?"

The thread of the story is immediately broken ; the witness's mind is carried back like a wounded soldier to the rear, and it is some time before he can be brought to the front again. Nor is this all. The judge is angry (if a judge can be), and the mind of the jury is prevented from following the course of the narrative. If the question be of importance, the judge's notes must be altered, and probably will be confused. Had the order of time been observed, the notes would have required no correction, and it is quite possible that the subsequent events take a different color from the answer. Besides this, the breach of this rule tends to multiply itself. The question having been interposed at the wrong time, the judge asks : " When was that said?" The witness becomes confused, tries to recollect, and very likely puts it in the wrong place after all, is reminded that that cannot be, is ordered to recollect himself and be careful, and so on, to the confusion of everybody except the opposing counsel, into whose hands the inexperienced junior is playing. It shows the necessity of

every event being placed in its natural order, and of every
material circumstance and conversation accompanying that
event being given in connection with it, so that everything
is exhausted as the story proceeds. If this be not done, the
client had better have been without your services.

*Let therefore the events be told in the order in which they
occurred, with the accompanying conversations, if important
and admissible, and their minor incidents if material.*

§ 23. *Repetition of Phrases a Fault.*—Another fault of
too frequent occurrence is the repetition of the phrases:
" You must not tell us what was said, but what was done."
" Did he say anything to you? Don't tell us what it was."
The jury, who know very little of the rules of evidence,
must sometimes think from the tone, as well as the language, that the counsel is afraid of something being told
that would be adverse to his case, and must wonder at an
advocate who asks if somebody said something, but
anxiously cautions the witness not to, tell what t was. It
may be said that the caution was necessary ; so it might be ;
but it need not be made the prominent feature in the examination. There need not be a fuss about it, as though you
wanted to impress the world with your vast knowledge of
the rules of evidence. In ninety-nine cases out of a
hundred, it is obvious that something was said ; the fact
will not be disputed, and a leading question will pass the
witness over the difficulty, and not confuse his mind by
sending it upon an inquiry as to why he must not give the
conversation.

Unless there be a doubt as to what an answer was, you
do not require it to be given twice. " Let well alone,".was
said by a judge to a junior, who was so enamored with a
witness' answer that he must needs hear it again and again.

§ 24. *Never Cross-Examine your own Witness.* — This
rule seems remarkably obvious. But it requires an effort
to obey it nevertheless. You will hear an advocate cross-
examine his witness over and over again without knowing

it, if he have not the restraining hand of his leader to check him.

Before Mr. Justice Hawkins, not long since, a junior was conducting a case, which seemed pretty clear upon the bare statement of the prosecutor. "Are you quite sure of so and so?" "Yes," said the witness. "Quite?" inquired the counsel. "Quite," said the witness. "You have no doubt?" persisted the counsel, thinking he was making assurance doubly sure. "Well," said the witness, "I haven't much doubt, because I asked my wife." Mr. Justice Hawkins : "You asked your wife in order to be sure in your own mind?" "Quite so, my lord." "Then you had some doubt before?" "Well, I may have had a little, my lord."

This ended the case, because the whole question turned upon the absolute certainty of this witness' mind. Of course, it is not suggested that a fact necessary for the ascertainment of truth should be suppressed, and in this particular instance the learned counsel was quite right in pressing the witness upon a material point upon which the prosecution rested ; but it is no part of an advocate's duty to endeavor to shake his witness' testimony to pieces if he believes it to have been honestly given. Nay, more. A cross-examination of one's own witness may most unjustly bring about a disastrous result. A witness may get confused, and although at first might feel absolutely positive, and be justly positive, yet, by the perpetually harassing him, he may begin to doubt whether he is positive or not, and leave an impression that he is doubtful. Such questions as : "Are you quite sure, now? Are you certain?" are cross-examination, and do not fall properly within the scope of an examination-in-chief.

§ 25. *Leading Questions.*—Leading a witness in material matters is a blunder which is not likely to be permitted by your opponent ; but if he do, it is generally a disadvantage. Evidence that is given in answer to leading questions is of the weakest character. The mere answers of a witness are nothing; it is the effect they have that makes them valuable or otherwise, and a jury always distrusts evidence which comes rather from the mouth of the counsel than that of the witness. As a matter of policy, therefore, apart from the violation of the rules of advocacy or the practice of the courts, leading questions upon material matters should be carefully avoided.

§ 26. *Examining from Brief.*—Except under particular circumstances, an advocate should not examine from his brief. The most complicated story is best unraveled in the ordinary and natural manner. Your brief is a statement of facts for your information, not for that of the witness. Let him tell his own story with as little interruption from you as possible, and in all probability he will tell it well enough if you do not confuse him with your brief. If you find he is omitting a material point, your duty will be to bring him to it at once.

§ 27. *Going too Fast.* — There is nothing more common with beginners than going too fast. They are frequently told by the judge that they forget that he has to take down the answers; and the importance of your evidence looking well on the judge's notes cannot be exaggerated when you are supporting or showing cause against a rule for a new trial. When the evidence is coming well, there is no doubt a great temptation to let it run too fast; but you must take care it does its proper work, otherwise it will be like a rush of water which shoots over the mill-wheel instead of turning it.

§ 28. *Keeping from Irrelevant Matter.*—But although it is by far the best to let a witness tell his story in his own way as much as possible, it is absolutely necessary to prevent him from rambling into irrelevant matter. Most uneducated witnesses begin a story with some utterly irrelevant observation, such as if they were going to tell what took place at a fire, they will say, " I was just fastening up my back door, when I heard a shout." But when you once get the witness at the scene, the evidence will come with little trouble.

§ 29. *Trifles may Turn the Case.*— Miracles are not common now-a-days, and events follow one another in a natural course ; and as one is often the cause and another the effect, the most important results may depend upon the merest trifle. Take the familiar "running-down case." Two vehicles come into collision, and the respective drivers no less so in their evidence. Each throws the blame on the other, and if both were believed, there could have been no accident at all, because each would have been upon his proper side of the road, close to the curb, with the whole width of the road between them. They cannot, therefore, both be accurate. Other witnesses give other impossible stories. The very position of the vehicles after the accident may be a disputed point, and, therefore, no assistance to the jury. But there may be a very trifling scratch or indentation on a wheel or a shaft which may be all-important, and what it was produced by may be more important still. Its direction and shape may also be material, and will show how necessary it is in examination-in-chief to get out every fact, however trifling, that may be of importance to your case. An instance of this kind occurred not long since, when a hansom cab, proceeding down Regent street, came in contact with a brougham which was crossing at right angles. The probabilities were all immensely in favor of the brougham. It was not likely the coachman would drive a valuable horse across a crowded street with such utter recklessness as to dash into a vehicle. The lady in the brougham said the cabman was inebriated ; the coachman said he was drunk : and the police who took him to the station charged him with being drunk and incapable. The divisional surgeon reported him as "the worse for liquor ; not unable to walk, but unable to manage a cab." This was an extremely strong case on the part of the brougham, and it was a serious one, as the valuable horse had to be killed on the spot. All the evidence was as conflicting and contradictory as to the accident as could well be, and to make it the worse for the cabman, the gentlemen he was

driving were not called to give evidence on his behalf. He
had to rely upon passing cabmen and the driver of a hearse,
who deposed as to pace. There was, however, in the midst
of all this confusion, one point of evidence which could not
be contradicted. The verdict did not depend upon the
"inebriety" or the "drunkenness" of the cabman, or the
pace of the cab, or the evidence of the witnesses, but upon
a small scratch which had been made on the off-side of the
cab by the point of the shaft of the brougham. On
this piece of evidence alone there was a verdict for the
defendant.

§ 30. *Interrupting the Witness.*— Another common error
is worth noting, and that is the not permitting a witness to
finish his answer, or tell all he knows on a material matter.
In the very midst of an important answer a witness is very
often interrupted by a frivolous question upon something
utterly immaterial. This seems so absurd on paper that it
needs an example: A witness is giving an answer when
some such question as this is interposed: "What time was
this?" or, "Had you seen Mr. Smith before this?" A
question is often left half answered by such interruptions,
the better half perhaps being untold. "He never asked
me about that," says the witness after the case is over; or,
"I could have explained that if he had let me." If the
question be material, by all means let the answer be taken
down; if immaterial, it ought not to have been asked; but
once asked, you had better have the answer, lest something
should be inferred against you.

§ 31. *How Not to Examine — Another Illustration.*— I
will give another instance how *not* to examine a witness. It
is an almost verbatim report of what actually occurred recently at a trial when an inexperienced junior was examining a witness.

Q.— "Were you present at the meeting of the trustees
when an agreement was entered into between them and the
plaintiff?—Answer, "Yes."

Q.—" Will you be kind enough to tell us what took place

between the parties with reference to the agreement that was then entered into between them?''

This is an instance of verbosity, which shows that in putting questions, long-drawn sentences should be avoided. The more neatly a question is put, the better, as it has to be understood not only by the witness, but by the jury. All that was necessary to be asked might have been put in the following words ;—

" Was an agreement entered into between the trustees and the plaintiff?''

" What was it?''

It will appear even more strange perhaps to the reader to say, that after the answer was given by one witness, which was all that was necessary to prove that part of the case, the question was repeated to another with additional verbiage.

" Will you be good enough to inform us what took place upon that occasion between the parties, as nearly as you can, with reference to the agreement that was then, as you have stated, entered into between them. Please tell us, not exactly, but as nearly as you can, in your own way, what his exact words were?''

It is obvious that if an advocate would take as much trouble to study advocacy as a boy does to learn the multiplication table, such a question would no more be asked at the bar, than a boy of twelve would find out how many nine times nine are by counting them on his fingers.

There is no doubt that the time of the jury is frequently wasted to an unwarrantable extent from a want of knowing how to examine a witness-in-chief. To frame a question well is a most important matter , and this can only be done by careful study. Practice alone is not enough, and indeed, will do very little towards effecting this object; it is more likely to confirm tendencies to verbosity than to diminish them. I am speaking now of length of questions, and not of the time in putting them. It is a very little fault to be slow in this particular, provided they are put well and

tersely.   It is a far greater fault, and a more dangerous
one, to be impetuous; more tantalizing to judge and jury,
and more ruinous to the interests of your client.   You had
better, if you have a case at all, be too slow with a witness
than too fast.   If his evidence be necessary, or, as is sometimes the case, unavoidable, you must call him; if called,
you should examine him as though you believed what he
says.   If you are afraid of the cross-examination, that can
be no excuse for slovenly and slurring examination-in-chief.
You need not cross-examine your own witness; but if you
are to examine him at all, do so boldly, and not as if you
distrusted him.   If in cross-examination he brings you to
the ground, the fault will not be yours.   You need not
blush to lose a case which your witnesses cannot support.
A worse thing may happen to a' client than losing a bad
case—he may win it.

CHAPTER III.—THE CROSS-EXAMINATION.

Next to examination-in-chief, nothing is more important or difficult in advocacy than cross-examination. It is infinitely the most dangerous branch, inasmuch as its errors are almost always irremediable. It is in advocacy very like what "cutting out" is in naval warfare, and you require a good many of the same qualities; courage with caution, boldness with dexterity, as well as judgment and discrimination. You must not go too steadily and with too direct a course, lest the enemy should measure your distance too accurately, and taking too steady an aim, sink you with a single shot. Nor must you loiter too long in a place. You must circumvent a good deal, firing a shot here and a shot there, until, maybe, you can catch your adversary unawares and leap on board. It has been likened to a two-edged sword, but it is infinitely more dangerous than that. It is more like some terrible piece of machinery — a threshing machine for instance — into which an unskilful advocate is more likely to throw his own case than his opponent's.

§ 32. *Dangers of Cross-Examination.*— It might be as well, before proceeding to discuss the qualities necessary for a good cross-examiner, to point out some of the dangers attendant on cross-examination. "With a view to practical utility," says Whately, "the consideration of dangers to be guarded against is incomparably the most important, because to men in each respective profession the beneficial results will usually take place, even without their thinking about them, whereas the dangers require to be carefully noted and habitually contemplated, in order that they may be effectually guarded against. A physician, who had a friend about to settle in a hot climate, would be not so likely to dwell on the benefits he would derive spontaneously from breathing a warmer air, as to warn him of the dangers of sunstrokes and marsh exhalations." The dangers of cross-examination, it may be observed, are so subtle that they lurk around the questions of the most skilful. These are like the marsh exhalations — invisible but destructive ; while there be often sunstrokes to which the most robust and vigorous often succumb.

These dangers will doubtless be guarded against by experienced counsel in every possible manner, and in most cases warded off ; nevertheless they are there, and what has been said as to the marks of a great general will to some extent equally apply to the advocate—"he is the greatest who makes the fewest blunders."

§ 33. *One Mistake may be Fatal.*— A mistake in cross-examination may be fatal to your case. A single question may make an opening for a flood of evidence which may overwhelm you. Suppose a conversation to have taken place which is not admissible as evidence in chief, but which, if admitted, may have the effect of prejudicing the jury, or of introducing matter otherwise irrelevant, but which, nevertheless, must in some degree influence their minds, it would be the height of folly to put a question which would admit it in re-examination. "Of course no one would think of doing it," is the obvious remark ; "there is no need to warn the youngest advocate against a danger so apparent." No one would *think* of doing it, but it is done unthinkingly every day, and is one of the most frequent blunders made by young advocates. It is a danger very often too obvious to be noticed.

In a recent case a plaintiff sued for several sums of money lent to the defendant during a period of five years. The justice of the claim to some or all of the several sums was in dispute. The man had advanced moneys. Whether he had lent all or not was one question ; whether he had been paid all that were admitted to have been advanced was another. The accounts were of the loosest possible kind, and it was obvious that a trifling circumstance might influence the minds of the jury. It was equally important on the one side to get in evidence for the purpose of influencing them and making them believe that all the moneys had been advanced and were unpaid ; it was equally the duty of the defendant, who believed he had not received some, and had paid the remainder (a certain sum having been paid into court), to shut out all that was not strictly in the nature of evidence. Now. it happened in this case (which was tried before Mr. Justice Denman) that the plaintiff had either kept no account books or had lost them. He depended upon his memory for his accuracy as to the various sums said to have been lent and for the dates, which were not only at wide intervals, but also, many of them, long ago. In examination-in-chief, he was asked if he had an account. He said yes. Made when? Some time ago. How made? From memoranda which were not in court. The account, therefore, was objected to.

Now it was quite possible, if that account had been placed before the jury, it might have wrongly influenced their minds, and it was right to shut it out. The plaintiff was thrown, therefore, upon the resources of his memory, and with regard to two items only, he was tolerably clear as to the dates and circumstances. In cross-examination he was asked, " Have you any account or memorandum showing the several sums you claim?" He said, " Yes, it is here," again producing the copy of his account. It was again

objected to. Question : " In what sums was it advanced?"
Plaintiff looked at his document and said, two sums of
twenty-five pounds each, and (*here he was stopped as he was
reading from his memorandum*). Plaintiff's counsel then
claimed that the document was in and could be shown to the
jury. Mr. Justice Denman held that it was not in evidence,
and that no question had been asked respecting its contents.

It will be seen from this — and one illustration is, perhaps, as good as twenty — that a single question in cross-
examination might have made that evidence, which by no
possibility could have been so made by the other side.

§ 34. *Strengthening Your Opponent's Case.*—Another
danger to avoid is that of strengthening your opponent's
case by eliciting answers that have more effect upon the
jury when they come by way of cross-examination than in
chief. A question is sometimes omitted fairly enough, and
for good reasons, by the counsel examining in chief. If the
cross-examining counsel be inexperienced, he will perhaps
rush in and get the answer for his opponent. The greater
weight attaching to it need scarcely be pointed out.

' Again, you may get in a conversation that may be fatal
to your case. Suppose the question to be the contents of a
lost will. A legatee under it gives the following evidence :
I remember the fact of the testator making his will. I saw
him writing it and I read it at the time. I was left a thousand pounds by it, and my two brothers were left severally
the same amount. I last saw the will two months ago.
Now, it might be that the whole case depended upon the
accuracy of the witness' memory, or upon that coupled
with his credibility. Plaintiff's counsel is desirous of showing that, on the day the will was made, the witness went for a
doctor, and told him, at that time, the contents of the will.
If this statement could be given, and it were identical with
that made in the witness box years after, it is clear that it
would go a long way to establish the accuracy of the witness's memory as well as his credibility. But it is not admissible as evidence in chief. A question, however, in

cross-examination would admit every word. Nor does the danger cease when this witness leaves the box. The doctor, a witness to the will, may be called. He may not have read it, but an inadvertent question may enable him to say what the last witness told him on the occasion in question.

§ 35. *Pressing a Reluctant Witness.*—There is another danger not to be lightly regarded, and that is of persisting in pressing a question upon a reluctant witness. When you find a witness unwilling to give the evidence you seek, and you have drawn him as near to the point as there is any hope of his being drawn or driven, it is always dangerous to attempt to urge him further. If you have nearly got an affirmative, and you press him over much, you may irritate him into giving you a direct negative.

The dangers thus indicated will doubtless suggest many others to a mind anxious to master the rudiments of advocacy. They can only be avoided by careful study. Practice itself is a slow teacher, and an unfortunate blunder may retard the advocate's progress in this branch of learning, and may lose him many a client.

Cross-examination may almost be regarded as a mental duel between advocate and witness. The first requisite, therefore, on the part of the attacking party (namely, the advocate) is a knowledge of human character. This is the first requisite, and it is an indispensable one. But as I suppose almost every one conceives himself to be a master of this science, and as, if he be not, it is impossible by any means at my disposal to add to his knowledge in that respect, I shall proceed on the assumption that the reader will appreciate many observations which would not be quite so intelligible were he ignorant of this profoundest of all learning.

§ 36. *Preserving your Temper.*—It will be clear that to cross-examine with anything like success, the most thoroughly good temper should be preserved. An ill-tempered advocate would be something like a jibbing horse, he would do everything but go along smoothly. On his hind legs (I

mean the advocate) in an instant. A calm, imperturbable
temper is the very triumph of self-command, and one of the
very foremost qualities of a good advocate. It is useless to
make excuses for a bad temper, as sensitiveness, indiges-
tion, or what not. Good temper is the demand of your
client, and in mere justice to him you are bound to preserve
it. Even if you should be a constitutionally irritable man,
you must absolutely conquer your irritability for the time
being. You must never even appear to lose your temper, for
no one ever believes that a man in the heat of temper means
what he says. Allowance is always made for this infirmity.
But when the jury have reason to make this allowance, the
chances are that your case is gone — in all probability your
client also.

Nor should it be forgotten that nothing more quickly manifests itself to the jury than a man's temper. It is almost
an instantaneous betrayer in the home circle. The smallest
child perceives it in a moment. It can not be disguised. It
is as perceptible as the effect of a sudden breeze passing
over a smooth lake. I would sooner have a cause fought
by a good-humored plodding advocate, than by a brilliant
and ill-tempered one. In the former circumstances, if my
case were good, I could scarcely lose it ; in the latter, it would
be almost impossible to win it.

§ 37. *Studying a Witness's Motives.*—Assuming, then,
that you have some knowledge of human nature, you will
be able to divine, while the witness is being examined in
chief, the kind of man you have to deal with. You will determine whether he has learnt his story by heart; if so, it
is probably not all true, especially if it be a long and intri-
cate one. This, however, is by no means an unerring test.
It may be true nevertheless. Many policemen learn their
evidence and give it off *verbatim*; yet it is more often than
not, substantially true. But you will gather from the witness's manner, his mode of answering, his looks, his tone,
his language, his very glances, whether he be a false witness

or one who is telling a story partly true and partly false, the most difficult of all witnesses to deal with.

But besides determining in your own mind whether he be false or true, or partly one and partly the other, you will also ascertain whether he has a strong bias one way or the other. If he have a strong leaning to the side of your opponent, you will have the less difficulty in disposing of him, because it will be easy to lead him on until his bias becomes so manifest and overpowering, that the jury will discount his evidence, and that to so great an extent, that if the case depended upon him they would throw it over altogether. A strong interest weakens the side on which it lies. It will, therefore, be clear that in cross-examining a witness of this kind it will be proper to elicit this at the earliest opportunity. If it comes last, it will be far weaker, because it will not altogether undo the effect which his evidence may have made upon the minds of the jury. The interest· a witness has in a case should, therefore, be shown early in the cross-examination, if it has not been made manifest before. Of course, your opponent will not leave you this card to play, if he can avoid it ; but he cannot help your overtrumping him by placing it more prominently before the jury than he would ever permit himself to do ; and this it will be your duty to accomplish.

But it may be the witness has no interest. He may nevertheless be a partisan ; and partisanship is often stronger than self-interest, although the latter has somewhat erroneously, as it seems to me, been described as the most powerful principle influencing human actions.

You may take it for granted that if your opponent should sometimes anticipate you in showing his witness's interest in a cause, he will never be eager to acknowledge him a partisan. You will, therefore. generally be left master of the field in this respect, and at liberty to choose your time, place, and mode of attack ; and so that it be early, you may do it as you like. In a great number of cases there is something of partisanship, and you may take it as a rule that an absolutely unbiased witness is rare. The strong partisan, however, is only produced by public questions, parochial disputes, boundary questions, quasi-political inquiries, medical cases, rating matters, running-down causes and other investigations, where the witnesses seem naturally to take sides. You should remember that though a man may go into the witness box under compulsion, he never gives his evidence without a motive. It may be a strong or a weak one, but it exists; find that out, and you will be able to do so if you watch and listen attentively. The man whose motive is simply to speak what he knows, manifests it in every tone, look and word. You will not have much difficulty in dealing with him. If you believe in your own case, you may believe in this witness not to injure it if you are discreet in examining him—that is, if you examine in such a manner that his answers cannot be misunderstood. But what are you to ask him? Listen to his evidence; if it agrees with your case, nothing; if not, note the points that are against you. And in dealing with the modes of cross-examining the different kinds of witnesses further on, I will endeavor to point out the manner of dealing with a witness who has a pure motive, but whose evidence conflicts with your case.

But suppose the witness has some other motive in giving his evidence. You will endeavor to ascertain what it is. If you watch minutely, you will find a difference in tone and manner when he is speaking more directly from the particular motive. Suppose it's revenge. Any point which seems more particularly to damage his adversary will be laid stress upon. Any answer that he makes which he thinks will damage him, will be uttered in a more ready tone and with evident satisfaction. It will manifest itself in his voice, in his look, and his whole demeanor. That, therefore, must be stamped upon the mind of the jury by your cross-examination. But there are subtle motives, by no means apparent to every observer, which will nevertheless be discovered if you set yourself to the task of finding them out. And whatever the motive be, there is some ground work for cross-examination, which must be clumsily administered indeed, if it do not in some measure help your case—*if you have one.*

§ 38. *When not to Cross-Examine.*—It is a good rule in cross-examining a witness, *never to ask a question the answer to which may be adverse to your case.* Nothing but absolute necessity should induce a departure from this. There are so many ways of framing a question or a series of questions, that it would disclose a poverty of ingenuity indeed, if you asked one that might involve the fate of your client. It may be said " every one knows that." True ; but strange enough, every one does not practice it. Junior barristers constantly put questions and elicit answers dangerous and often fatal to their case ; whereas, with the exercise of a little ingenuity, they might, by small portions at a time, as if they were enticing a shy bird with crumbs, obtain little by little that which they require as a whole. Too little attention is paid to small matters in advocacy, the minutest point being frequently the pivot upon which the whole case will turn.

But when you have once got the whole, remember that you can have no more ; and whether it comes to you in crumbs or slices, avoid placing the whole before the witness, otherwise you may yet succeed in getting it denied in the lump, besides being involuntarily led into an argument with the witness. If the series of answers lead irresistibly to one conclusion, that conclusion will be obvious to the jury without directing the attention of the witness to the fact.

But not only when you are doubtful of the answer, should this course be adopted, but even *when it is necessary to your case that a particular answer should be obtained.* And I would suggest it as a good and safe rule, that if you are desirous of getting an answer to a particular question, do not put it. The probability is that the witness will know your difficulty and avoid giving you exactly what you wish. If not altogether straightforward (and for such witnesses you should always be prepared) he will be on the alert, and

unless you circumvent him, will evade your question. It is
in such a situation as this that the skill of the cross-examiner is shown. One advocate will sit down baffled, another
will obtain all that he requires. A series of questions, not
one of them indicative of, but each leading up to the point,
will accomplish the work. If the fact be there, you can
draw it out; or if you do not so far succeed, you can put
the witness in such a position that from his very silence the
inference will be obvious.

One of the greatest cross-examiners of our day advised a
pupil, in cross-examining a hostile witness upon a point that
was material, to put ten unimportant questions to one that
was important, and when he put the important one to put it
as though it were the most unimportant of all. "And
when," said the learned gentleman, "you have once got
the answer you want, leave it. Divert the mind of the witness by some other question of no relevancy at all." There
is no occasion to emphasize an answer while the witness is in
the box, if it be properly put. The time for that will come
when you may sum up or reply. If the witness sees from
your manner that he has said something which is detrimental to the party for whom he has given his evidence — unless
he be an honest witness — he will endeavor to qualify it,
and perhaps succeed in neutralizing its effect. If you leave
it alone, it may be that your opponent may not perceive its
full effect until it has passed into the region of comment.
Nothing is more unskilful than repeating a question when
you have obtained a favorable answer.

Counsel are sometimes so impetuous in cross-examination
that they put two or three questions in rapid succession
without waiting for an answer, as though they were administering interrogatories. This is an exuberance of inquisi-
tiveness which must be restrained, if you really desire to
cross-examine with success.

Besides avoiding the danger of eliciting evidence which
may be adverse to your client, it should be remembered that
by cross-examination a color may be given to that elicited

in chief, which may not only emphasize it, but *give it the appearance of evidence which you yourself have adduced.* Counsel should carefully avoid making his adversary's witness his own by cross-examination, as he certainly will if he obtain answers favorable to the other side.

It is a good rule *never to put a question in cross-examination without being able to give a reason for it.* Many young advocates rise to cross-examine without the least idea of what they are going to ask, and take the witness back through the evidence-in-chief, as though it had not made effect enough upon the jury. Nothing can be more unskilful than this. " Cross-examination," said a learned judge to a junior, " does not consist in repeating in a louder tone the examination-in-chief." This is simply the result of inexperience and a want of knowledge of the fundamental principles upon which an advocate should proceed. It is true he soon learns that it is necessary to have an object in asking a question ; but in giving these hints I am desirous of his learning it at once, without the painful experience which comes of many blunders.

Another atom of advice I would venture to give, is *not to cross-examine for explanations,* unless the explanation is necessary for your case. No doubt there is some degree of fascination in solving a mystery, but when you find that the explanation of it is immensely to your disadvantage, you will not quite so much enjoy the quiet smile of your opponent when he finds that you have cleared up something which he could not, and which he has purposely left for the exercise of your ingenuity and fertility of inquiry. If you don't know whether the ice will bear, you had better not venture on it.

It must not be forgotten that apart from the nature of the questions, the *tone* in which they are asked will not only have a great effect with the jury, but with the witness himself. A cross-examining counsel should always seem in earnest ; if he have the appearance of one who is simply

endeavoring to amuse an audience, the jury will quickly
come to the conclusion that he does not believe in his own
case. From first to last, and in every stage of the case,
you must make it appear that you really believe in the cause
you are advocating. You may not, in reality, have much
faith in it, but your own opinion may be wrong; and as you
are representing the interests of another, you must, at
least, appear to be serious. Manner plays a great part in
advocacy. Every one knows that a question in one tone
will induce an answer, wherein another it will not; that
the emphasis upon a particular word may produce a totally
different version from that which it would cause if laid
upon another. But no one can lay down a general rule on
the subject of style. You cannot make an orator by advice, or a skilful advocate; the most one can hope for in
giving hints is to assist young advocates in developing the
powers they possess, and in pointing out certain dangers to
be avoided.

§ 39. *Conclusion.*—That the modes of cross-examination
which I have enumerated are useful, is a matter not of
speculation, but of experience; that they may be useful to
others, I have no reason to doubt. Many of these hints
may appear to be commonplace suggestions, but it is nevertheless true that commonplace ideas more often than not
come to us only after long experience or through the kind-
ness of an experienced friend. Many come after wearying
disappointments and heartfelt rebukes. I have noted these
down with the hope of saving some the weary and watchful
labors that so many have undergone. I have nowhere
attempted to throw out a hint for the purpose of enabling
an advocate to confound or entrap the honest and truthful
witness, around whom every protection should be thrown;
but my endeavor has been to suggest modes of dealing with
the artful and the vicious, in order that deceit should be
baffled and imposture exposed. Having said so much, I
would add another word. Having studied your hardest to

learn how to cross-examine, your next lesson should be how to do as little of it as you can ; you should never cross-examine if you can safely avoid it, and when you do, let your questions be few and with a purpose. *The best cross-examiner is generally the shortest.*

(4)

CHAPTER IV.—The Classes of Witnesses.

From the subject of cross-examination to a study of the various classes of witnesses who may become the subjects of that ordeal, the transition is natural. It is superfluous to say that the variety of characters which may be displayed in the witness box is almost infinite ; for the supply is drawn from the inexhaustible reservoir of human nature itself. The witnesses however, most usually encountered in practice, may be classified under the following heads : The lying witness ; the flippant ; the dogged ; the hesitating ; the nervous ; the cunning ; the hypocritical ; the witness partly false ; the positive witness ; the stupid ; the truthful ; the expert witness ; the *non mi ricordo* witness ; the bully ; the swift witness ; the female witness. More than one of these characters are often united in a single person ; for man, even in the witness-box, is prone to " play many parts." Every witness performs at least two characters—one on the direct, the other on the cross-examination. The lying witness lies straight through, but on the cross-examination superadds the characteristics of the dogged or the flippant

witness to his original *rôle*. The witness, swift on his examination-in-chief, is dogged or bullying when cross-examined, and so with most of the others. The only fixed exception is that *rarissima avis*, the strictly and absolutely
impartial witness, always upright and downright, whose
judicial mind will not permit him to waver a hair's breadth
toward one side or the other.

§ 40. *The Lying Witness.*—A witness whose evidence is
untrue must lie with wonderful skill if he go through even
his examination-in-chief without betraying himself. He is
the easiest of all to dispose of, and, once discovered to the
jury in his true character, will do more harm to a cause than
half-a-dozen truthful witnesses will undo. The greatest instances in modern times of this class of witnesses were the
notorious " claimant " and his supporter Luie. I may here
remark that the Tichborne trials will well repay a careful
perusal ; for they afford illustrious examples of every
branch of advocacy, and are a mine of inexhaustible wealth
to the aspiring advocate. A lying witness, however, is
not always to be disposed of by a flourish of the hand,
but in most cases, if you. have had any experience, you will
be able to refute his statements by his own lips.

He comes up with a well-concocted story, and tells it
glibly enough. Now you are well aware that events in this
world take place in connection with or in relation to other
events. An isolated event is impossible. The story he
tells is made up of events which, if true, fit in with a great
many other events, and could not have happened without
causing other events or influencing them. If his story be
untrue, the matters he speaks of will not fit in with surrounding circumstances in all their details, however skilful
the arrangement may be. The multitude of surrounding
circumstances will all fit in with a true story, because that
is part and parcel of those circumstances carved out from
them ; just as the oddest shaped stone you could cut from
the quarry would fit in again to the place whence it was taken.
It is, therefore, to the rock, of which it once formed a part,

that you must go to see if the block presented be genuine
or false. You must, in other words, go to the surrounding
circumstances. The witness, however clever he may be,
can not prepare himself for questions which he has no conception will be put to him, and if you test his imaginary
events by comparing them with real events, you will find
the real and the false could not co-exist in their entirety ;
there must be a displacement of facts that have actually
occurred, which is impossible.

Will a lying story fit in? It is certain it will not ; but it
may not be possible to obtain an accurate view of the surrounding circumstances — that is the principal difficulty.
But you may almost always get at some of them, and these,
however few, will answer your purpose. In cross-examining
a witness who lies, you must therefore apply the test of
surrounding circumstances, and compare his testimony with
that of other witnesses. The latter will be the severest and
the surest test, if you apply it to the smaller details. It
need hardly be said, that the greater the number of witnesses
to prove a concocted story, the greater the certainty of ex-
posure by a skilful cross-examiner. The main facts of a
story may be so contrived as to be spoken to by all the witnesses ; but they can not agree upon details which never
occurred to them, or concoct answers to suit questions of
which they have no conception.

But even in this mode of cross-examination you must be
careful not to obtain an apparent corroboration, where you
seek contradiction. The way to avoid this is not to put the
same question upon some important piece of evidence to every
witness. If you have got the first contradicted by the second,
let the matter rest ; the next witness will make a guess and
corroborate the first, which will materially weaken the effect
of the contradiction. By judiciously pursuing this line, you
may get all the witnesses to contradict one another. It was
the great complaint of Brougham, in Queen Caroline's trial,
that the story was so well concocted that two witnesses were
never called upon one important fact. This, of course, was

contrived so that there should be no possibility of contradiction. It is not difficult, if there are several witnesses
telling an untrue story, to break them down in cross-examination; and one of the best instances I have met with is that
narrated in the story of Susannah and the Elders. This
example of cross-examination further shows how necessary
it is that the other witnesses should be " out of court," while
one is under examination.

It is when you have to deal with an untruthful witness
who speaks only to one set of facts, and stands alone with
regard to that evidence, that your skill is put to the test.
How are you to shake his testimony? Assuming that character is not altogether out of the question, you will ascertain who he is, and upon this point he may not be touched;
he will, probably, if a stranger, be prepared with an answer
which will render futile all further inquiries. If you know
the witness is a man of bad character (that he has been convicted, say), your task will be comparatively easy. But
even then, if you are not prepared to contradict him by
legal evidence, he may defeat you by indignant denials.

It may be said, "Everybody knows that." True; but even
in putting questions as to a witness having been convicted,
there is all the difference in the world between one mode
of putting them and another. If you do it unskilfully, the
effect of the surprise on the jury may be lost, and in advocacy surprise is a powerful emotion to enlist on your side.
An advocate who can surprise either a witness, or a jury, or
his opponent by a question, is a formidable adversary; but
you may so unskilfully put your question as to evoke sympathy on behalf of the witness instead of contempt; whereas,
if your questions are well asked, you may not only show that
he is not to be believed on account of his previous character, but also on the ground that his mode of answering condemns him as a false witness. You may get his conviction,
in short, and a lie at the same time, which will be a good
measure of his character for the jury.

" For bringing to light the falsehood of a witness," says
Whately, "really believed to be mendacious, the more
suitable, or rather the only suitable course, is to forbear to
express the impression he has inspired. Supposing his tale
clear of suspicion, the witness runs on his course with
fluency till he is entangled in some inextricable contradiction, at variance with other parts of his own story, or with
facts notorious in themselves, or established by proofs from
other sources."

If you know nothing as to character, you must proceed to
test him by surrounding circumstances, leading the witness
on and on, until, encouraged by his apparent success, he
will soon tell more than he can reconcile, either with fact
or with the imagination of the jury. At a trial at Warwick
some years ago, a remarkably well-planned *alibi* was set up.
The charge against the prisoner was burglary. An Irish
witness was called for the defense, and stated that at the
time the burglary was committed, the prisoner was with him
and four or five other persons some miles from the scene of
the crime. The time of course was a material element in
the case, and the witness was asked how he fixed the exact
time. He said there was a clock in the room where he and
the prisoner were, and that he looked at it when they went in
and when they left. He was then told to look at the clock
in the court and say what time it was. The witness stared
vacantly for a considerable time, and then said it was
" such a rum'un he couldn't tell."

" Can't you tell a clock? "

" Shure, sor, I cant't tell that un !"

What was still more strange, the same question was put
to every witness, and there was only one out of some six
persons who could tell what o'clock it was. And yet they
all swore to the exact time deposed to by the first witness,
and repeated the answer as to how they knew the exact
time. Of course the *alibi* was totally broken down, and
the prisoner was convicted.

Give your liar plenty of line, and you will find that his tale of lies will be proportionately great. A mile with him will become three, if you let him think your object is to make it less. Darkness will become " light as day," and the moon will shine with the utmost splendor when, according to the almanac, she is nowhere. It is impossible to tell how far the downright liar will go if you only give him a little encouragement. You may not be able to contradict him upon all points, but this benefit always accompanies his evidence, that exaggeration, as a rule, requires no contradiction. Let him exaggerate and color to the full extent of his inclination or imagination, and when he has completed the picture every one will see that it is a monstrosity, in other words, no one will believe a word he says. "A liar is not to be believed, even when he speaks the truth." It is an old saying, but will never be so old as to be worthless.

But you may get an actor in the box, who for a long time will conceal his true character. He may be a man who has a spite against the plaintiff, the defendant, or the prisoner, as the case may be. Or if none against the parties to the action, he may have a very strong feeling against some person interested in the result of the case. If you would cross-examine to any effect, this must be ascertained. It is the very point, remember, which he will conceal if he can, but it is also the very one that you must find out and expose. You will probably detect it during the examination-in-chief, if you are vigilant; if not, it must be ascertained in cross-examination. I would ask you to bear in mind, while on this subject, that if you want to read a man's real character, you must look at his mouth; all the other features may, to a certain extent, be controlled; but the mouth never can be sufficiently to conceal the emotions from a quick observer. All the passions seem to play upon the lips ; and if you question the witness suddenly and somewhat sharply upon the subject that is really most strongly operating upon his feelings and inducing his evidence, you will perceive the involuntary motion of the mouth, which will instantly betray him.　A beard, even, can not altogether hide this wonderful index of the mind.

Dickens, in his magnificent "Tale of Two Cities," says: "Any strongly marked expression of face on the part of a chief actor in a scene of great interest, to whom many eyes are directed, will be unconsciously imitated by the spectators."

So, if you direct a witness's attention to those facts in connection with a case which you suspect have strongly roused his feelings against the plaintiff, defendant, or any other person interested in the proceedings, you will gather from the involuntary expression of his features whether you are correct in your surmise; and what is of still greater importance, the jury will perceive it as well, after you have followed up your question by another and another, for ultimately concealment will be impossible.　This is part of what is called "the demeanor of a witness," so often spoken of as of such inestimable importance as one of the tests of a witness's truth or character, so highly appreciated and yet so little understood in its subtler significance.

It might be here observed, that whenever you have once caught your witness, do not lose the benefit of the capture by exhibiting him too ostentatiously.　You need not give him a second run for the purpose of going over the same ground again.　Having got the answer you want, keep it, and at once go off upon another point; otherwise, if you get him to repeat it for the purpose of directing attention to the good point you have made, he will qualify what he has said, and very likely unsay it altogether by some lying explanation.

§ 41. *The Flippant Witness.* — When a witness comes into the box with what is commonly called a "knowing" look, and with a determined pose of the head, as though he would say, "Now then, Mr. Counselor, I'm your man, tackle me," you may be sure you have a FLIPPANT and masterful being to deal with.　He has come determined to answer concisely and sharply; means to say "no" and

" yes," and no more; always to be accompanied with a lateral nod, as much as to say, "take that." But although I have used the male pronoun, the witness is very often a female. She has come to show herself off before her friends; she told them last night how she would do it, and feels quite equal to " any counselor as ever wore a wig." "She'd wig him, she would." No doubt this would be quite true elsewhere—but in the witness-box! You must demolish her, my friend. There's a life and death struggle in this cross-examination; but you must win.

I have seen many a counsel put down by such a witness; a sharp answer, with a spice of wit in it, has turned the young advocate into a blushing boy, and utterly discomfited him. Perhaps a laugh has been caused by some impertinent observation. The best advice under these circumstances is, first of all, to make up your mind not to be put down. No matter what happens, you will sit down the winner. But you must preserve the most placid and unruffled demeanor, and above all things, never reply upon the witness. To be led into a retort, unless it were an absolutely crushing one, would betray a weakness, and show that the witness was making the running, not you. To argue with a witness is not only to abandon your high post of vantage, but to make a bad impression on the jury. You are no longer the advocate, but are reduced to the level of an ordinary disputant. Argument is not cross-examination; the time of incubation is not yet. You will be able to see what you will make of the evidence by-and-by; at present it is your duty, by questions, to get as much as possible in your favor, or to destroy as much as possible that which has been given against you.

In dealing with this class of witnesses, an advocate should carefully abstain from administering any rebuke, or attempting " to put the witness down." His object should be to keep her up as much as possible, to encourage that fine frenzied exuberance which by-and-by will most surely damage the case she has come to serve. A little encourage-

ment will be of more service to you than anything that
would tend to damp the ardor of this flippant fury. Besides, you will have the opportunity of animadverting upon
her evidence by-and-by, and then you will be enabled to
show by the contrast of a quiet manner with her blatant and
irrepressible demeanor how utterly worthless her evidence
is. Any good effect which any portion of it may have
produced will share the condign fate of the remainder.

And it should not be forgotten that contrast invariably
has a striking ·effect with hearers. It produces a feeling
akin to that of surprise ; and whenever this is effected, it is
in favor of the advocate who can produce it.

But there may be a point or two which you may be
anxious to elicit, even from a witness of this class ; for
although her evidence on behalf of the party for whom she
is called may be comparatively if not entirely worthless,
whatever may be elicited on your own behalf will have an
importance in proportion to the degree of hostility manifested. This not only shows the danger of calling any such
witness, but also the necessity of taking every advantage of
the occasion when she is called. I will endeavor to point
out the mode of putting a question in such a case. You will
always approach her as if she were a wild animal, ready to
tear you if she could get you near enough. Therefore, circumvent. You may be sure she will never give an answer
that she supposes may be favorable. It is necessary, therefore, to watch for a fitting opportunity, and if you allow
her to make some particularly good hit against you which
causes a laugh, she will be in an ecstacy of triumph. And
at the moment of her triumphant excitement is the time to
put in your question ; but it must not be done as though
you thought it a matter of importance, but rather as though
you were putting it for the purpose of turning off the laugh
against you. While off her guard, if your question be well
worded, the answer will slide from her flippant tongue
before she is aware or has had time to consider its effect.
But having got it, pass away from the subject instantly by

putting another question of no importance or relevancy
whatever. This is a hint for which I am indebted to an
esteemed friend, who thinks the proper study of an advocate is advocacy, and who found in repeated instances that
this mode was pursued by one of the greatest cross-examiners of our time. It has also been confirmed by my own
observation. You will find your advantage in this witness's
triumph.

§ 42. *The Dogged Witness.*— The dogged witness is the
exact opposite of the one I have just been dealing with. He
will shake his head rather than say no. As much as to say:
" You don't catch me. You see him, gentlemen, and you
see me. I'm up to him." He seems always to have the
fear of perjury before his eyes, and to know that if he keeps
to a nod or shake of the head, he is safe. He is under the
impression that damage the case he must, whatever he says.
" A still tongue makes a wise head," has always been his
maxim. How are you to deal with him? If he has said
nothing against your case, you will of course leave him
alone—always, unless you wish to draw something from him
in its favor. If you cross-examine at all, you must beware
of letting him think that you have any design of " catch-
ing him." Most witnesses think this. And such a witness
as we now have, looks upon the learned counsel about to
cross-examine him with similar feelings to those of the
little boy whom a big boy kindly asks to be permitted
to " show him London ; " a personally conducted tour
which consists in the person showing, holding the boy heels
upwards until the tourist declares he sees St. Paul's. In-
sinuation will help you with this witness. But carefully
avoid asking for too much at the time. Get little answers to little questions, and you will find as a rule that
answers are strung together like a row of beads within the
man ; and if you draw gently, so as not to break the thread,
they will come with the utmost ease and without causing
the patient the slightest pain. In fact, till he hears you

sum up his evidence, he will have no idea of what he has been eased.

This witness, without being untruthful, is always hostile ; he looks on you as a dangerous man, a sort of spy. He will become bolder as he proceeds, especially if you prove to him that you are by no means the terrible man that he at first thought you. And the best way to foster this idea is to accustom him to answer. Let him see that your questions are of the simplest possible kind ; even so simple and so easily answered that it seems almost stupid to ask or answer them. "Of course," he says to one ; "Certainly," to another ; "No doubt about that," to a third, and so on. Presently you slip one in that is neither "of course" nor "certainly," and get your answer. He may be an old man (generally is), and the subject of inquiry a right of way. He may be the "oldest inhabitant." What are the moving springs of human conduct? Love of justice, which he has known from a boy upwards, and his father before him, as "right is right, and wrong is no man's right." Self-approbation, or vanity, which in him signifies "a wonderful memory," which has been the talk of the neighbors for years. The knowing more of by-gone times than any man or woman in the place. Selfishness, called by him his "uprightedness and downstraightedness ;" independence of spirit — "he cares for no man, and always paid twenty shillings in the pound." These are the vulnerable points in his armor ; and if you can not thrust an arrow in at any of these, you had better hang up your bow, for you will never make a good archer. He will answer anything if you appeal to his memory, or if your question magnifies his independence of spirit, or brings out in all its dazzling luster his "uprightedness and downstraightedness."

§ 43. *The Hesitating Witness.* — A hesitating witness may be a very cautious and truthful witness, or a very great liar. You will find this out before you begin to cross-examine. In most cases the hesitating man is considering what effect the answer will have upon the case, and not what the proper answer is. By no means hurry this individual; if he is balancing the merits of the case and the weight of his answer, and the scale it should go into, give him time, and in all probability he will put it into the wrong one after all. If he should, leave it there by all means. I advise this, because I have so often seen young advocates take it out again and put it into the other. Besides, your giving him plenty of time will tend to confuse him—as confused he should be, if he is not honest. He can't go on weighing and balancing effects without becoming bewildered as to their probable results. Nor is there any danger in being slow with this witness; he must be a much sharper man than you, and must know better than you what is passing in your mind, if you do not at last contrive to land him in an unknown region where perchance there be giants, hobgoblins, and what not.

But your cross-examination should by no means lag on his account, nor should its pace slacken. Slow questions are usually feeble. With this witness they should be asked at the ordinary speed, or if anything, perhaps a trifle quicker, so that the hesitation may be more apparent and the blundering more complete.

§ 44. *The Nervous Witness.*—A nervous witness is one of the most difficult to deal with. The answers either do not come at all, or they tumble out two or three at a time; and then they often come with opposites in close companionship. A "Yes" and a "No" together, while "I don't know" comes close behind. "I believe so," or "I don't think so," is a frequent answer with this witness, as it is with the lying and the truthful witness. They are all partial to this expression, but all from different and opposite motives.

You must deal gently with this curious specimen of human nature. He is to be encouraged. It is no use to bray him in a mortar. Counsel often get irritable and petulant, and ask such questions as these: "Pray what do you mean?" "You say yes and no in the same breath." "Will you be good enough to explain to those gentlemen what you mean?" This is bad, and "those gentlemen" generally dislike the soft sawder implied. Some counsel may not know it, but the fact remains that they injure their clients by observations of this kind. Besides, the rebuke and the oblique flattery to the jury do not produce the effect of restoring the witness to firmness or self-possession. You should bear in mind with this as with all witnesses, that the smallest point you can extract in your favor is worth all the trouble you may be put to in obtaining it. You should deal as gently with a weakness of this kind, as you would with a shying horse; pat him and humor him, while you accustom him to face the dreaded object, which is your learned self. The nervous witness, like all others, is either to be cross-examined or not; if he be, you must do it without driving him into such a state that his answer, however favorable, will have no value in the eyes of the jury; and this will surely be the effect of your agitating him in the manner indicated. Endeavor to quiet his nerves if you think you can obtain anything from him that may serve your case; if not, leave him alone altogether.

§ 45. *The Cunning Witness.*—The cunning witness must be dealt with cunningly. Humor would be mere pastime, and straightforward questioning out of character with him. But by way of contrast, and for that only, straightforwardness may not be out of place with the jury. Whatever of honesty, whether of appearance, manner, tone or language, contrasts with the vulgar, self-asserting, and mendacious acting of this witness, will tend to destroy him. It will be the antidote to his coarse poison. It is strange but true, that no man can be what is usually understood as a "cunning person," and conceal the fact. He is not really a shrewd man, but only thinks he is, tries to be, and above all, wishes to be thought so. He always pretends that he has some deep and hidden meaning in what he says and does, which no amount of skill or perception on your part can penetrate. He would be an impostor to the world if he could, but the only person he really imposes upon is himself. Every one can see that he tries to appear what he is not, and that he pretends to know a great deal more than he does. This is the man to show to the jury in his real character. But it by no means follows that, if you do, they will disbelieve him altogether. They will discount his evidence, and without some corroboration attach little weight to it. If contradicted by a respectable witness or a fact on your own side, they will discredit him altogether. You will, therefore, leave him to himself; he will exaggerate and color in his own vulgar manner, utterly unable to perceive that he is producing a distorted account which no one will believe.

If you get this witness laughed at without appearing to design it, he will be at your mercy, for vanity is his moving spring also; and although he is vain of those qualities which most men despise, he is still vain and desires to be thought clever. To be laughed at for a fool, therefore, will be beyond endurance; his temper will be lost, and his cunningly devised story and impudent repartees will lose their effect. But the laugh should appear to be the result of an accidental surprise; something that he has brought upon himself, and not that you have designed for him.

§ 46. *The Hypocritical Witness.*—The canting hypocrite is not the least pleasing object of creation when in the witness-box, nor is he the most difficult to cross-examine. He invariably speaks from the very best and purest of motives. His desire is only to speak the truth; no, not merely that, but without so much as an apparent tinge of partiality. He has no interest in the case — no feeling. It is such a pity it could not have been settled out of court as he proposed, himself to be the arbitrator.

Here is a good man for you. It is almost a pity that necessity and a sense of duty should compel you to cross-examine such a man at all. It seems almost an insult, but it is excusable on this ground — that his extreme disinter-

estedness and impartiality might impose upon the jury, and
do your client an injustice if you did not.　Now you will
observe about this rogue that whenever he approaches a
downright lie he shirks it.　It is a part of his very character
to believe he is an honest man.　When he comes to a lie,
therefore, that he dare not face, he is like a bad hunter who
will not leap the fence, but looks round to see if there be a
gap somewhere hard by, or a somewhat lower fence that he
may scramble over, and so not do violence to himself in the
event of a mishap.　The hypocrite coming up to the lie,
says : "I am not quite clear ; I should hardly like to go as
far as that."　But he will wriggle over on to the other side
somehow, if you show him a place.　So if you put it to him
something in this form : "I presume I may take it, Mr.
Pecksniff, that so-and-so is the case?"　"Well, I think you
may."　Now he is fairly over.　You will not fail to mark
this characteristic in him, that whenever he begins to think,
to be not quite sure, not clear, and to believe, and presume,
and so forth, he is incubating a downright lie.　He himself
is a lie that needs little telling.　His evidence, which may
and will be always on the confines of truth, must be closely
examined to see on which side of the boundary it really is.
If it be on that of falsehood, it is so very near the truth that
you can scarcely distinguish the dividing line, and if it be
on the other side, it is equally near a lie.　But you can make
his evidence valueless by pushing him over sometimes on to
the side of truth, and sometimes to that of falsehood.　He
balances himself so nicely that a finger's touch is sufficient
to disturb his equilibrium, and if he do not always go over,
the jury will perceive his grotesque efforts to keep his position.　A persuasive tone and manner, somewhat assimilated
to his own, as though you were conscious that you had to
deal with a very good and amiable creature, who could not
possibly be made to lie even by means of thumbscrews and
iron boots, and who would rather be torn to shreds with wild
horses than swerve from his integrity, is the most effectual
mode of dealing with this witness.　He is too excellent to

deny the truth if you put it to him in infinitesimally small quantities at a time, in the shape of simple leading questions, each one carrying with it the shadow of perjury, which this man will always avoid committing at any cost.

§ 47. *The Witness Partly False.*— The witness who is partly true and partly false, without hypocrisy, knowing that he is giving color to some facts, suppressing others, and adding little ones to make good measure for his party, is the most difficult of all to deal with. The process of separating the true from the false requires skill as well as ingenuity and patience. You must have a delicacy of touch in manipulating evidence of this kind, that comes only by actual practice. Experienced advocates are frequently deceived, and judges even fail at times to separate what is true from what is false. As some diseases are beyond all the remedies in the Pharmacopœia, so this kind of witness is beyond the reach of any one faculty the advocate can bring to bear upon him, and sometimes defies the skill of all the qualities combined. Tact, ingenuity, patience, perception, judgment, experience, are all requisite in the highest degree in dealing with this witness. And you must bear in mind that it is not sufficient for yourself to know the nature and character of the evidence; your task will only be half accomplished at this point. There will still remain the more difficult one of exhibiting it to the jury in the same light, and with the same aspect with which it presents itself to your own mind. The jury, untrained to sift evidence, will not so readily detect imposture and deceit as you; nor will they so easily distinguish between what is true and what is false, when the ingredients are mixed up cunningly in the evidence of an artful witness of this description.

If, however, you can lay hold of any one part and expose an incongruity or an incompatibility, you will have accomplished a great deal. Expose an attempt at deception anywhere in a witness's evidence, and you have nearly, if not quite, destroyed it all. You must watch carefully to find

(5)

out if there be a want of assimilation in the parts of the
story; if there be a disagreement between some of the false
parts and some of the true; you must ascertain if such a
series of facts can naturally exist together and in connection
with one another, and must cross-examine for causes and
effects, so as to determine if these agree with facts stated
by other witnesses. Men do not gather " figs of thistles,"
and if you find the same cause producing opposite effects,
there is falsehood somewhere.

Improbabilities always have great weight with a jury;
and if you cross-examine for these in a witness who tells a
story partly true and partly false, you may succeed in de-
tecting some. Of course, much that has been said with regard to the mode of cross-examining one witness will apply
to others; and it may be that, apart from showing the in-
trinsic weakness and improbability of the story as a whole,
you may be able to break the witness down altogether, by
showing that he is quite unworthy of belief. If so, you
need cross-examine no further, unless you desire to contradict him by evidence on your part.

The story told by this witness would resemble a neatly
papered wall. On a general glance, such as an ordinary
spectator would give, it would appear perfect; but a critical
examiner would discover that the pattern was broken here
and there to meet the requirements or shape of the wall,
notwithstanding that considerable skill had been employed
to make the broken portions fit in so as to deceive the eye.
As a whole it looks complete; examined in detail, the
patchwork is apparent; the pattern is not preserved in an
integral condition.

§ 48. *The Positive Witness.* — There is another class of
witness which may be mentioned, and that is the positive
witness (generally a female or of female tendencies). It is
usually very difficult to make the witness unsay anything
she has said, however mistaken she may be; but you may
sometimes lead her by small degrees to modify her statements, or induce her to say a great deal more in her posi-

tive way; and the great deal more may be capable of contradiction, or may itself contradict what has been said before by the same witness. If you deal with her skilfully, she will in all probability be equally positive about two or three matters which can not exist together. She is the worst witness to unsay anything, but the best to lead into a contradiction of what she has said.

§ 49. *The Stupid Witness.*—Another class of witness not unfrequently met with in court is the stupid witness. There are many kinds of stupid witnesses; but the particular specimen upon which I would fix the reader's attention is that civil and agreeable being who agrees with everybody for fear of disagreeing. He belongs to no exalted rank in society, you may be sure, and is not assisted in his worldly pursuits with a superabundance of the highest intellect. Enough, perhaps, to enable him to currycomb a horse or wheel a barrow. It is of no use whatever to manipulate this evidence into downright contradictions. The jury will put down one-half of the result to the advocate's ability, and the other half to the witness's stupidity, and unless other reasons intervene, will credit the first account given by him and laugh at the rest.

This witness is respectful to a fault, and that fault is timidity. Suppose the action to be for trespass and injury to a horse, and the statement of claim alleges that the defendant wrongfully took a horse belonging to the plaintiff, out of the plaintiff's stable, and rode it for a long distance at full speed, whereby it became broken-winded and useless. Defense: permission to ride the animal when not required by the plaintiff; riding in accordance with permission, and denial of improper pace, broken-windedness, and so on. Sprouts, the "odd man," is called for the plaintiff, and says he found the stable door open and the horse gone. He "never gave no leave to take it, and the horse came back all in a lather and broken-winded like." Now Sprouts is not so much actuated by a desire to tell the truth, as by a wish to be agreeable all round; Sprouts is a man of the world, and desires to offend nobody; above all, desires to keep his place. Since the day he interposed his friendly offices between Todd and his wife, he has never interfered in other people's business, and would not have come here to-day if he had not been obliged. You cross-examine him as follows:

"It was a fine morning, I think you said, Sprouts?" "Yes sir," says Sprouts.

"Not *very* wet, was it?" "Not *very*, sir."

"What you call muggy, I think — damp and close?" "It was, sir."

"The sort of weather to make a horse perspire a good deal?" "Make him what, sir?"

"Perspire." "Prespire! yes, it would, sir; it would that."

"I believe the horse has not been clipped?" "No, he haven't sir."

"He would naturally get warm?" "He'd smoke a bit, sir."

"I think you smoke, Sprouts?" Sprouts is in a cloud at once — enveloped — you can hardly see him; but what you do see of him is grinning with the utmost civility.

"Sometimes, I suppose, Sprouts?" — the more you "Sprouts" him, the more agreeable he becomes.

"Were you smoking at the time the plaintiff came up to you?" "I believe I was, sir."

"And did he not say he was sorry he had given the defendant leave to take the horse, as he was such a regular madcap he didn't know where he'd ride him to? Set a beggar on horseback, he'd ride to——Well, we won't mention names, Sprouts. Did he say that?" Sprouts laughs through the smoke, and begins to rub his cheek.

"Did he say so?" "Something of the sort, sir," says Sprouts.

"Did he say that?" "Not all, sir."

Judge: "Which part did he not say?" Sprouts forgets what the question was.

Counsel: "Did he say the part about madcap?" "He did, sir."

"And that he was sorry?" "He was terrible sorry, sir, sure enough."

"And do you mean to say, Sprouts—will you pledge yourself he did not say, he was sorry he had given him leave to take the horse, or words to that effect?" "I won't say he did, and I won't say he didn't. I won't tell no lie if I knows it."

"I don't pledge you to the very words, Sprouts; but I ask whether he did not use words to that effect?" That last "Sprouts" was so in accordance with the native civility of the witness, that he strokes his chin tenderly, and says—"He might."

This is not a far-fetched specimen of the evidence of the genus "Sprouts." But a cross-examination which leads to such results is useless. The jury will take the evidence in chief as true, and will not accept seriously the answers elicited by such a mode of questioning. I have many times seen it fail in the cases where weak and stupid witnesses have been examined. The line to take is not that which leads this kind of witness into mere inane contradictions of all he has said before. With a sharp person this would result in the overthrow of the evidence altogether. Not so, however, with that of the stupid witness.

Now suppose you have had a quiet conversation with him, just by way of getting explanations of various things he has said, you will both have enjoyed the few minutes of pleasant intercourse. Just as you are about to part, in fact, as you are sitting down, as a sort of " bye, bye, Sprouts" you bethink you of the question, " *The horse is not a ich damaged, I hope?* " — " No," says Sprouts ; " he's all right now."

In the case I have supposed, the last answer of the witness must be taken to really represent the fact. There is a way of reserving *the* question you wish answered till your witness is in the humor to answer it. Most friends are amicable when they part.

§ 50. *The Truthful Witness.* — The truthful witness has been said to be the most difficult of all to cross-examine. I can not help differing so much from that opinion as to say that I have always regarded him as the easiest of any. When I say truthful, I do not intend to imply that his evidence is necessarily true. If it were so, it would be idle to cross-examine at all. What I mean by a truthful witness is one who believes and intends his evidence to be true. He is the easiest to deal with, because he does not equivocate or prevaricate. He has no secret meaning, and gives his answers readily and without mental reserve. He desires to tell you all he knows, and his credibility, I will assume, is unimpeachable.

The first thing to ascertain in cross-examining a witness of this class, is whether he has any strong bias or prejudice in the matter under inquiry. One or two carefully worded

questions will discover this, if you have not already learnt
it from his answers in chief. Suppose, for example, he is a
clergyman, and the question is as to a certain place of en-
tertainment being a nuisance, either as being badly conducted or conducing to immorality. He tells you truthfully
enough what he has seen, and speaks with indignant or pathetic tones of the vicious example to the inhabitants of the
neighborhood. In his evidence in chief he will speak in
general terms, probably, and not descend to particular
instances; but you will learn by closely watching, whether
he has any particular examples of debauchery or profligacy
to depose to. I do not mean that you are to draw these
from him if he have any; this, of course, you will carefully
avoid; but if he has not referred to particular instances, you
may safely proceed to lead him to condemn all places of
public amusement of a similar kind. If you lead him
gently, he will follow with remarkable docility. I have seen
this course pursued by eminent leaders with great success.
A man who condemns all alike is not the witness to impress
a jury with the value of his evidence in the particular instance, especially where it is far more a matter of opinion
than fact. Even fact itself may be represented as so shocking by a witness of this kind, as to create laughter instead of
indignation. I once heard a highly respectable and pious
individual tell a bench of magistrates at quarter sessions,
that all dancing licenses ought to be taken away because
they prevented gentlemen from getting good housemaids.
A gentleman described the conduct of two individuals as
debased and disgusting; when questioned as to what they
were doing, he said with great solemnity " he saw the man
kiss the girl and hold her hand." On being asked if he
had never been guilty of similar conduct in his earlier days,
he declined to answer, and amid an outburst of laughter
said, " But the girl was a Sunday-school teacher." This
not being enough to produce the horrible effect he antici-
pated, he threw into the scale, as a final circumstance of

depravity, the fact that, at the time, the young man was paying his addresses to another young woman.

An instance of a witness being broken down in cross-examination by a single question occurs to me. She was doubtless a truthful witness, and desirous of telling all she knew. Her daughter, the prosecutrix, had charged a man with rape. Her evidence, from some cause or other, was unshaken, or at all events not sufficiently so to break down the case for the prosecution. She denied everything that could cast a doubt upon her own conduct, and spoke positively upon every point that told against the prisoner. The mother was then called to prove that the prosecutrix had promptly complained of the prisoner's conduct. She was cross-examined as to whether her daughter had not made similar complaints to her about other men. She said "Yes, sure she had; she were always complainin' o' bein' raped by one and t'other of 'em, and that was why she brought the prisoner up; she wur determined to make a sample o' one on 'em, and wanted to show 'em as they must leave her alone." It was as much the manner of putting the question which drew this answer, as the mode in which it was framed, which was so effective.

A truthful witness may be called to give evidence, let us suppose, in a "running-down" case, and may state positively what he saw. It is almost too obvious to remark that you must cross-examine as to his exact position, the moment as to when his attention was called to a particular occurrence, his opportunities for observing what took place, as to when his attention was subsequently called to the matter, what was said, and in what way his mind was directed to it — in short, you will test his memory and his accuracy. It will be strange if he be not brought into collision with some other witness equally accurate but with no less a tendency to blunder, or with some material and perhaps undisputed incidents of the occurrence; and though ever so truthful, he may be utterly broken down.

Sometimes a truthful witness will unconsciously color a

transaction, if he be closely connected, either by relationship or friendship, with a party to the action; and this is highly important to remember in cross-examining a truthful witness.

It frequently occurs that some circumstance is omitted in the examination in chief (and this should always be watched for), which, if supplied, would give a totally different aspect to the transaction; and this may be the case with regard to the effect producible on the minds of the jury, when it would be otherwise as to the mode in which it would operate upon that of the witness. As you can never tell what point may at any time influence a jury, it is safe to say that you ought to elicit every circumstance that can not operate to your prejudice. A witness's appreciation of the matters he speaks to is often extremely important to ascertain. He may utterly fail to understand the bearing of his own evidence, and may give a totally erroneous and misleading version of the facts, often mistaking his own construction of them for the events themselves.

§ 51. *The Expert Witness.* — The rapid march of science and improvement has developed a type of witness that in the earlier history of the law existed only in a rudimentary condition, — the expert witness. *Cuique in sua arte credendum est,* is the maxim upon which it is predicated; and the great increase and infinite variety of this class of testimony are proof alike of the material progress of the country, and the facility with which the administration of the law adapts itself to new conditions. Almost all questions now admit of expert testimony, and every grade of professor, from the scientific savant and high art *dilettante* to the humble corn-doctor, depose professionally in court, and opound *ex-cathedra* theories and systems. The expert witness differs from the ordinary witness in that the latter must state facts only; whereas, it is the function of the former to express opinions, based, however, *solely on the facts developed by the evidence,* and in these opinions consists the value of his testimony. With this sort of personage, especially the higher scientific variety, the lawyer is at a serious disadvantage. The witness is also a professional man, professor of a science of which the counsel necessarily knows little, and in point of fact seldom knows anything whatever. He stands before the learned pundit " overpowered by a jargon more mysterious than his own," in a bewilderment not unlike that of Meg Merrilies, the gypsy fortune-teller, in the presence of Mannering and Dominic Sampson, as they discoursed with grave erudition on astrology.

As to the examination or cross-examination of an " expert," it is the duty of the counsel to see that the opinion of the witness is based upon the *facts* that have appeared in the evidence ; for these are the symptoms which it is his function to diagnose. Experts of every variety have pet crotchets, theories and systems, by which they are exceedingly prone to solve all knotty questions that may be presented in their art or science, and this they do in perfect innocence unless restrained by the watchfulness of the court or counsel. The chief advice to be given to the advocate on this subject is of a retrospective character. Try to have already learned as much as possible of the art, mystery, or science of the deponent, and particularly of that branch of it which affects the matter in controversy. "A little learning is a dangerous thing," no doubt; but in such a matter as this, contrary to Pope's assertion, no learning at all is still more dangerous. At the very least you should have so far mastered the definitions and technical terms, that you can officiate as interpreter between the jury and the witness ; for the erudite man will assuredly deliver himself in the language of his calling, in " words of learned length and thundering sound." Most sciences, be it remembered, are as rich in technical terms and as little to " be understanded of the people " as the law itself. A diligent preliminary coaching, therefore, will place you in a position approximating in elevation the pinnacle upon

which the witness stands, and probably above that occupied by your "learned friend on the other side."

There is a class of lawyers, patent lawyers and the like,
who make a specialty of some particular branch of learning, a sort of combination lawyer-scientists or scientist-
lawyers, to whom these observations do not apply, except
indeed when they stray beyond the limits of their bailiwick.
It sometimes happens that (outside of this class) the counsel himself is an "expert" as well as the witness, and the
advantage he obtains is very notable.   Professor Greenleaf
in early life was indoctrinated in the mysteries of ship-
building, which was his father's business.   While at the
bar, he chanced to be retained by an insurance company to
defend a suit for injuries to a vessel which at the time was
lying at the wharf.   The question was narrowed to this;—
if the damage was to the bottom of the ship, it was within
the policy, and the company was responsible; if to the side
of the ship, it was caused by negligence, and the company
was not responsible.   A builder testified that the injury was
to the bottom of the vessel, and that he had furnished the
timber with which she had been repaired.   Upon cross-examination he was asked by Mr. Greenleaf—

"In building a vessel, after laying your keel, you secure to it with
iron bolts a row of crooked timbers—floor-timbers, eh?"

Ans. "Yes."

Question. "Then comes a series of timbers called futtocks — is that
so?"

Ans. "Yes."

Question. "The next above is called a rising timber — is it not?"

Ans. "Yes."

Question. "The next is the naval timber,— and the next still the top
timber — is that correct?"

Ans. "Yes."

Question. "Now — on your oath — was it a floor timber, a futtock, a
rising timber, a naval timber or a top timber, that you furnished to repair that vessel?"

Witness, reluctantly. "It was a naval timber."

This answer demonstrated that the vessel was injured in
the side, and Mr. Greenleaf gained his case because he

knew the details of the business on which the issue depended.

If, however, you have not the advantage of being an expert yourself, it is well, in examining or cross-examining an "expert" witness, to bear in mind Hamlet's advice to the players, to speak no more than is set down for them. It is dangerous to travel outside of the record. Cleave to the scientific issue; for if you deviate from the prescribed course, you will assuredly flounder into deep water and come to grief.

The most usual variety of the expert witness is the medical man. The doctor, like the poor, we have always with us. Like bad luck (and very much like it), he is everywhere. He administers the first soot-tea to the ailing and wailing infant, and the last hopeless anodyne to the departing graybeard. Of course, courts of justice cannot escape his ubiquity, and there he very often delivers opinions of the very highest importance, involving the lives, characters, and fortunes of the parties to the suits in which he testifies. The range of subjects which fall within his province is almost as wide as that of the ills to which in his regular business it is his duty to minister. Legitimacy, age, identity, life insurance, mental alienation, with all its multitudinous problems and puzzles, feigned diseases, malpractice, death natural or violent, suicide, murder, poisons in all the infinite complexity of toxicological science—upon any or all of these grave matters, the medical witness may pronounce opinions which are justly entitled to great weight. So close is the connection of the legal and medical professions, growing out of these subjects, that the science of Medical Jurisprudence, or, more properly Forensic Medicine, has developed from the numerous points at which they come in contact. A diligent study of the authorities of this conjoint profession ought to enable the lawyer to intelligently examine or cross-examine the doctor on medical points, and the doctor not only to deliver his testimony with "good emphasis and discretion," but to know something of

the nature of legal evidence — what it is proper for him to
say of his own motion, what he should only disclose in answer to authorized questions, and what he should retain in
the great store-house of his knowledge. How far Medical
Jurisprudence is understood by the average lawyer or doctor, it would be invidious to inquire ; but whosoever, of the
legal profession at least, may be conscience-stricken or
humiliated by his ignorance on this subject, may take com-
fort from the fact that if he knows anything whatever
about it, he knows a great deal more of it than did the
great lights a hundred or so years ago. In the first of his
lectures, delivered in 1758, Blackstone cast a sort of
dragnet into English society, demonstrating that each class
ought to study more or less law, and why duty and interest
required it at their hands ; but he could think of no other
or better reason why the medical gentleman should know
any law, than that it would be well for him to understand
how to draw a will — deprecating in advance, however, the
obvious gibe that the probate of a will was the logical
sequence of the attendance of a physician. (1 Black. Com.,
p. 14.) It seems never to have occurred to him that as
surgeons and physicians constantly testify professionally in
the courts, it might be well for them to learn a little of the
laws of evidence and of those laws which govern questions
of mental alienation, crimes and criminal proceedings.
Nor, on the other hand, did he think to advise the law
student in view of possible future use to acquire a smatter-
ing of Pathology, Anatomy, Physiology and the like. The
lawyers of his day did not know the *cerebellum* from the
patella, nor the *cutis vera* from the diaphragm.

The medico-legal learning of the average American lawyer is usually a faint reminiscence of the law school, or a
mere modicum gotten up *pro re nata*, and consequently he
stands in slippery places whenever he is required to conduct
or defend a case which may depend on medical testimony.
So far as the medical phase of this matter is concerned,
"they manage these things better in France." As early as

1606, King Henry IV., of France, directed his chief physician to appoint two surgeons in each city or large town,
whose duty it should be to examine and report on all
wounded or murdered persons, and from this nucleus grew
up the system of French Medical Jurisprudence.

The great difficulty with medical testimony is, that it so
often gives an uncertain sound. That " doctors differ " is
proverbial. The science is not an exact one. Medical
gentlemen, although honest, intelligent and impartial, are
prone to cherish crotchets, to be sometimes dogmatic and
didactic, and withal to indulge freely in a most pedantic
use of technicalities, disregarding the advice of Sir W.
Blizzard, who in one of his lectures adjured them to " be
the plainest men in the world in a court of justice."*
Hence it is not wonderful that they frequently get up medical questions more doubtful, perplexing and complicated
than the legal issues on trial. In addition, there is a pro-
lific cause of disagreement in the fact that they are usually
required to hear testimony on the facts ; to draw, without
time for consideration, professional inferences from that
testimony, and pronounce at once a medical opinion upon
it. Beck complains (2 Beck Med. Juris. 912), of the delivery of the testimony as to the facts *viva voce*, and says that
it is the most common cause of the disagreement of physicians in their opinions of such facts. He is right, no doubt.

---

* The proclivity of medical men to use *hors de propos* of technical language is amusingly illustrated by the following anecdote :

"I discovered considerable *echymosis* under the left orbit, caused by
extravasation of blood beneath the cuticle," said a young house surgeon
in a case of assault at the assizes.

Baron Bramwell: "I suppose you mean the man had a black eye?"—
Scientific witness: "Precisely, my lord."

Baron Bramwell: "Perhaps if you said so in plain English, those gentlemen would better understand you?" " Precisely, my lord," answered the learned surgeon, evidently delighted that the judge understood his meaning.

This would have been worthy of the young saw-bones who described
a suppression of perspiration as "an agglutination of the sebaceous
follicles."

With a mass of testimony, confused and contradictory, a
number of medical witnesses in a cloud as to what has been
proved and what has not, two or more lawyers who do not
understand the physicians, it is hardly reasonable to expect
that the jury, however sensible, could evolve order out of
such chaos.

All this should impress the advocate with the absolute
necessity of understanding his case beforehand, and especially the medical phase of it.   If you go to trial imper-
fectly prepared on the law of the case, you can possibly
worry through safely by virtue of your reserved fund of
legal lore stored up in your memory, which may providen-
tially be brought to your aid at the critical moment; but in
this extra-professional matter you have *no* reserved fund—
you know nothing whatever concerning it, except what you
have learned for this express purpose.

If that is inadequate, you are without remedy.

§ 52.   *The non mi ricordo Witness.* — There are two
varieties of the witness who has forgotten things; one is
wicked, the other is weak.   The former cannot remember
this, that or the other circumstance adverse to the cause
which he has espoused, but his memory is clear as to the
other facts of an opposite tendency.   Several notable historical specimens of this class figured in England upon the
trial of Queen Caroline before the House of Lords in 1820.
They were Italians, and their formula *non mi ricordo*,
which, upon cross-examination, was used profusely, passed
for a season into common speech to designate the deponents
whose memory is so conveniently at the disposal of the
party which they favor.   The type is by no means extinct,
and still frequently appears on the stand.   Witnesses are
daily adjured to remember; to *try* to recollect something
which counsel especially desires to put in evidence, and on
the other hand the *most scathing and indignant comments
are made* upon the partiality of the memory which recalls
so many things—all of a kind, and refuses utterly to produce anything whatever—of another kind.

The exhibition of infirm memory, by a person otherwise sound mentally and physically, is phenomenal, and is in itself a badge of fraud, so to speak, authorizing suspicion and placing the witness under a cloud. It is hardly less to his discredit than self-contradiction, and when it is developed that the witness's memory is not only infirm, but very capricious and partisan, the presumption against his credibility becomes almost conclusive. There is no special mode of treating this sort of lying witness, except to press him hard, draw from him as many *non mi ricordo* answers as possible, so that you can argue from them that he, who has forgotten so very much, is not entitled to credit when he asserts that he remembers anything whatever. The jury may thus be induced to read his testimony, as the witches say their prayers, backward, and conclude that the circumstances so unaccountably forgotten are facts, and those so distinctly remembered are fabrications.

The witnesses who are innocently of infirm memory are timid, cautious, conscientious people, deeply impressed with the solemnity of an oath, determined to make no mistake, and yet committing a very grave one. They are resolved to do their duty, but fail utterly to perceive that their oath requires them to tell the whole truth, and they ignore the saving expressed in the formula, "to the best of your knowledge and belief." They cannot remember on the witness stand many things of the truth of which, everywhere else, they could not be more fully convinced if one should rise from the dead to confirm it. Such witnesses are of little value, and fall ready victims to the truculent cross-examiner.

§ 53. *The Bullying Witness.*— In the backwoods, rural districts, and new settlements of the United States, and sometimes in the older sections of the country, the advocate encounters another variety of witness — the bullying witness. He is usually a coarse, ignorant and violent man, deeply imbued with the vulgar prejudices against the profession, and fully convinced that the principal employ-

ment of lawyers, and their chief delight, is by artifice
to entrap into contradictions the witness whose misfortune it is to fall into their clutches,— or failing that, to
browbeat and terrify him into such a course of testimony
as will suit their nefarious purposes.   When it becomes
necessary for such a man to testify in a court of justice,
being combative by nature and habit, he takes the stand
with a certain grim joy ; for like the war-horse he snuffeth
the battle from afar, and he resolves at the very least to
give the " whipper-snapper " lawyers as good as they send,
to talk back as saucily as he likes, and to hoist the engineer
by his own petard.   Upon his examination in chief, if he
has a partiality for the side which calls him, he is quiet
enough ; but upon cross-examination his peculiar qualities
are fully developed.   Having very little respect for the
court, and none whatever for the bar, he holds his temper
under very slight control, and soon passes from sulky im-
pertinence into downright insolence and insult.   He considers it a great feat to bully a lawyer, and nothing restrains
him in the slightest degree, but judicial interposition which is
often tardy and only partially effective.   Under these circumstances the position of the advocate becomes trying.   It
is absolutely indispensable for him to control his own temper, which is a very difficult feat for the young and excitable,
and to make the most of the brute rage of the witness, ex-
tracting from him such admissions, concessions, or contradictions, as under the circumstances may be possible.   By
no means should the advocate answer in kind the violent
language of his adversary.   He should confine himself
strictly to the business in hand, maintain the most frigid
deportment, freeze out the bully, and impress him. if possible with the idea that in bearding a court of justice he is
incurring a very formidable and mysterious danger.   Old
stagers manage this sort of thing easily enough ; but the
fledgelings of the profession are often flurried by the violent
demeanor of the witness, lose their self-possession, and
sometimes let valuable points escape them.   This sort of

witness differs from the flippant witness in that he is a physical force, knife-and-pistol sort of man, ready for a fight, and desirous of an actual personal encounter with the disciple of Themis if he can find or make an available *casus belli*. He was formerly quite common in his appropriate *habitat*, but is becoming rare. Wherever he flourishes, his existence is a reproach to the judicial functionaries whose laxity of discipline renders him a possibility.

§ 54. *The Swift Witness.* — The swift witness is the partisan. For him the lawsuit has all the attractions of a horse-race or an election, and his devotion to the plaintiff (or defendant, as the case may be) surpasses that of the ward politician for the candidate of his and the people's choice. His devotion may be created by actual personal or pecuniary interest in the result, or friendship for one party, or hostility to the other, or all combined. Being an ardent and impulsive person, the swift witness is indiscreet ; nobody can moderate his zeal, and he enters the witness-box, as a knight prances into the lists to do battle *a l'outrance* in the cause which he has espoused. The swift witness rarely appears in an uncompounded condition, for man seldom performs any but the simplest actions from a single motive. Besides the great characteristic idea, there are ancillary impulses and habits which impart their color to the actions, and render man a morally variegated and composite being. The swift witness is often also a lying witness, or a positive witness, most generally the former ; for whenever strong partiality coincides with a feeble moral sense, the temptation to actual falsehood is likely to prove too strong for that sort of " poor, weak human nature." An amusing instance of this combination occurred recently in Maine. There was a suit instituted by a man for a divorce, and a witness who had testified strongly in favor of the husband was turned over to the other side for cross-examination. How far his zeal served his friend, will appear by the following colloquy :

" You say that Mrs. B. had a very retaliating disposition?"

(6)

"Yes, sir; that is what I said."

"Well, how did she retaliate? Give me an instance."

"I have told you once; she was always retaliatin'."

"Exactly; but we want a particular instance. Now look; did you ever see Mr. B. kiss his wife?"

"Yes, sir."

"And what did she do?"

"*She retaliated immejitly.*"

"That will do; you may stand aside."

§ 55. *The Female Witness.*—A woman on the witness stand is always, in insurance language, extra-hazardous. She is very rarely indifferent to the result of the trial, indeed, is usually partisan in her feelings, and often a "swift" witness of the most pronounced type; for women, as a rule, are not gifted with judicial minds, and lack the great juridical instinct of impartiality. If she favors your side, you will need all your tact, acumen and delicacy of touch to restrain her impetuosity, and prevent her from seriously damaging your case by her manifest bias. If she is against you, and it becomes your duty to cross-examine her, you labor under one disadvantage. She is protected by her sex from several lines of treatment usually considered admissible in other cases. You must in any event, and at all hazards, scrupulously preserve the *suaviter in modo,* and treat her with the most distinguished consideration. It will *not* do for you to lose your temper, or to give way to sarcasm, to bandy words, or otherwise manifest the slightest failure in courtesy. Such a course would assuredly enlist against you the chivalrous feeling of the jury, and possibly of the court itself. However voluble she may have been on her examination in chief, to you she will be curt and laconic, and you can only lead up carefully, slowly and insidiously, *per ambages,* to such admissions and qualifications of her direct testimony as may favor your views, and especially, with great care, encourage her to display, as conspicuously as possible, her prepossessions in favor of your adversary. Unless you are maladroit, or she unusually suspicious, you will succeed; for such cases are often exceptions to the Scriptural rule: "Vainly is the net spread

in the sight of any bird." If by this strategy you can secure some modifications of her testimony, and fully demon-
strate to the jury from the lady's own lips that you are not
in her " good books," you should be content and draw off
your forces. A partisan female witness is of very ques-
tionable value to the party which calls her, and if the cross-
examination be discreet and skilful, will count a point
against her friends, not in their favor.

But there are other women unlike this woman ; for,. Mr.
Weller's opinion to the contrary notwithstanding, all women
are *not* alike. These other women are timorous souls, who
have a most vivid idea of the pains and penalties, temporal
and spiritual, incident to the crime of perjury, and a fixed
determination not to incur them. They are so upright that
they lean over. Their exceeding caution often encumbers
their testimony with a multitude of provisos, saving clauses,
exceptions, and qualifications ; and unless by the address of
the examining counsel some stamina of fixed fact can be
inserted into the limp mass, their evidence, which might
otherwise have been valuable, becomes utterly worthless.
When such witnesses fall into the clutches of the cross-
examiner, they are as clay in the hands of the potter.

CHAPTER V.— THE RE-EXAMINATION.

This branch of advocacy will not require very elaborate treatment. Not that it is by any means an unimportant subject or a small matter in the conduct of a case ; on the contrary, it is worthy of the most careful study, and the following hints may be of some use, while they show the dangers as well as the advantages of re-examination. If it were not necessary, cross-examination would be useless. To restore the ravages that have been made by that destructive engine, is the principal duty of this portion of the advocate's work.

§ 56. *Effects of Cross-Examination.* — If you have watched the cross-examination with that unceasing vigilance which you ought to have bestowed upon it, you will have observed and noted the points that have been made against you. Some of your evidence has disappeared altogether ; other portions have received such a shock that they exist in a very rickety and dilapidated form ; some other parts have received a coating of interpretation, if I may use the expression, which must be removed ; other fragments lie here and there in a mass of confusion from which they must be extricated if you desire to re-establish your case. A hur-

ricane seems to have swept over your homestead, destroying
some of your less substantial outbuildings and threatening
even the mansion-house itself. In such a state of affairs
as this you will find much to do, and where to begin is the
first question. At the beginning, I would say, as nearly as
you can. Begin to repair where the first breach was made.
The witness may have given an answer he did not intend,
and very much of the subsequent mischief may have flowed
from that unfortunate mistake. If, therefore, you set that
right, you will easily pass along and repair the damages
which have resulted from it. Strict order and arrangement
in this branch, as in all others, should be observed ; everything done by design, and nothing left to chance. Proceed
in your work of repair as the destroyer proceeded in his
task of destruction. Explanations in this stage of the case
often make your evidence the stronger for the confusion in
which it has been temporarily involved.

§ 57. *Do not Re-Examine unless Necessary.*—But unless
re-examination be absolutely necessary it should never be
used. It is not every trifle that should induce you to commence afresh with your witness. If a trivial and unimportant point has been made, but the leading facts of the case
are left undisturbed, leave the matter to the jury. But the
point may be small, and yet not unimportant. Its position
may give it effect. By not re-examining when you are not
obliged to, the danger of cross-examining your own witness
will be avoided. You are not required to explain everything. It sometimes happens that a witness, from natural
suspicion of the intention of the cross-examining counsel,
will not answer intelligibly, will hesitate or stumble. It is
not, however, necessary that you should fly to pick him up
before he is down. If his evidence in chief has been fairly
given, the jury will be sure to make allowance for subsequent manœuvres to upset him. Whereas if you rush to
the rescue unnecessarily, and endeavor to obtain explanations not vouchsafed to your opponent, the witness will
think you are anxious for his answers, and recovering from

his nervousness, will fill up the gaps your opponent has left. In other words, you will complete his cross-examination, with this additional advantage to him, that the evidence will look like evidence in chief, and not like that extracted by a hostile examiner.

If an answer be elicited in cross-examination which is favorable to your case, it is highly important that you should not appear to be so fascinated with it as to re-examine upon that. Something else may be admissible in consequence, and this opportunity should be watched for and seized. If you re-examine upon the very fact obtained for you, this result may follow, that your opponent, who discreetly enough declined to pursue the subject further, may have the satisfaction of hearing you get an explanation which may neutralize the effect of his mistake. *"Leave well alone."* An answer favorable to you, elicited in cross-examination, is not a subject to re-examine upon of itself, but to be made the most of in your reply.

§ 58. *Rules for Re-examination.*—As you watch carefully the cross-examination of your witness, you will probably be made aware for the first time of many weak points in your case. If there should be one which you have flattered yourself has been passed cleverly by in your examination in chief, you may certainly anticipate a well-directed blow in *that* quarter, at all events. You must watch, therefore, like a second in a pugilistic encounter; for when it comes, your witness will in all probability require picking up. How to do it is more than I can tell, as I am not holding your brief, and know nothing of the facts. It is in the remedying of such a misadventure that the art of re-examination consists; and it is only by an intimate *knowledge of your facts and their relative bearings* that you will be enabled to set your witness up when his evidence has been thus battered.

Sometimes a cross-examination has been so effective that the evidence of a particular witness has been hopelessly demolished. An experienced advocate, under such circumstances, will resign him to his fate. If he have other witnesses upon whom he can rely, his task will be with them; if not, the case must fall with the witness.

Next to carefully watching for any points that may be made against you, a no less important duty will be to see *how you may turn any answer to your advantage.* Your adversary may not be a very skilful or experienced advocate; he may be an indifferent cross-examiner; in which event you may safely trust him to play into your hands. He will get portions of conversations which will make the remainder admissible; perhaps put in documents which will give you the same advantage, besides affording you the right of reply; and if you have been considerate, you will have left him to follow up a question or two put for the express purpose. This does not imply that you will have left anything out in your examination in chief which it was material to prove; that would be the height of folly. You must always assume that your opponent will not prove your case for you. I speak only of matters which you yourself can not get in, and which may, nevertheless, have an important bearing upon your case.

You must watch, also, to see whether any attack be made upon your witness in cross-examination. If his credibility be assailed, you must be prepared to re-establish it, if necessary; for that is the foundation upon which his evidence rests; and you must do it by questions that will elicit explanations of circumstances left doubtful, by removing the grounds of suspicion, and giving the real character to a transaction capable of two constructions. When this is properly done, nothing is more effective with a jury; they will feel as though they had been relieved of a burden. They will be pleased to find suspicion removed from a person whom they desire to believe; and not only this, the impression of having been imposed upon will also be removed, and their minds, temporarily disturbed, will settle down, as it were, into a state of tranquillity and satisfaction.

§ 59. *Evidence as to Character—An Effective Re-Examination.*—Cross-examination as to character is at most times an uncertain performance. You never can be sure as to the view the jury will take. It is the part of an advocate's duty which they least like. A personal suspicion arises that their own characters would not be secure from attack, if once they were compelled to enter the witness-box. Every delinquency might be laid bare, and his most tender feelings outraged by an unscrupulous and unfeeling advocate. All this might be quite unfounded as a suspicion, but that matters little if the suspicion exists. I need not say it is your bounden duty to protect your witness to the utmost of your power. Sometimes you may do it by way of objection, but if not, you must exercise your best skill to effect your purpose by re-examination.

I will give one instance where character was once in my hearing cruelly assailed in cross-examination by an inexperienced advocate, and upon whom it recoiled with crushing severity. He asked a witness if he had not been convicted of felony. In vain the unfortunate victim in the box protested that it had nothing to do with the case. "Have you not been convicted of felony?" persisted the counsel. "Must I answer, my lord?" "I am afraid you must," answered his lordship. "There is no help. It will be better to answer it, as your refusal in any event would be as bad as the answer." "I have," murmured the witness, under a sense of shame and confusion I never saw more painfully manifest. The triumphant junior sat down. Not long, however, was his satisfaction. In re-examination the witness was asked: "When was it?" A. "*Twenty-nine years ago!*" The Judge: "You were only a boy?" Witness: "Yes, my lord." It need scarcely be added that a just and manly indignation burst from all parts of the court, and the comments of the learned judge were anything but complimentary to the injudicious advocate.

§ 60. *Dangers to be Avoided.*—*Sometimes a question will be put in cross-examination which produces an answer not unfavorable to either side, b it which it may not be eonsidered safe to follow up by another.* You will have to consider whether it will be safe on your part to take it up where your opponent has left it, and you will best consider this by weighing the whole of the facts of your case and the effect of the answer whatever it might be; or you might put a question or two by way of test, and then abandon it or not, as the answers warranted.

Again, your opponent may have put a question which has "let in" something for you in re-examination; or, on the other hand, he may have put one which tempts you to follow it up, and by that means may have let you in. The utmost caution, therefore, is necessary in pursuing anything that has been started for you by your adversary. He is by no means a safe guide to follow, and the less you keep company with him, the better.

It might be observed here that one should not be too ready to object to questions put by way of cross-examination. *Sometimes they are asked for the very purpose of inducing you to object,* and when this is the case, and you fall into the snare, it is obvious that an unfavorable effect will be produced by you on the jury. They imagine at once that there must be something in the background which you are endeavoring to conceal. You lose their confidence, and in all probability rouse within them a feeling that they are being imposed upon and deceived.

When questions have been asked as to character and have failed, it is far better to deal with the matter in your address to the jury, than to put the stereotyped question in re-examination: "Is there any pretense for suggesting?" etc. The first denial answers all purposes for the time being, and the mere repetition of it adds no weight; besides, the natural indignation arising from the circumstance will be all the better for not being exploded too soon. A quiet and indignant protest to the jury will be all that is necessary. Above all things, it should be remembered, that *re-examination does not consist in repeating the evidence in chief, or*

in explaining answers that are in your favor.   If your case
be a good one, and your witnesses honest, very little will be
left to do at this stage of the proceedings.   If it be a bad
case, and your witnesses the reverse of truthful, all the re-
examination in the world will not set them up as they were
before.   It is of immense importance, and indeed necessary
for the purpose of explaining something which has been left
obscure; or removing an erroneous impression, or supple-
menting some matter which, taken by itself, looks to your
disadvantage ; for most other purposes it would be worse
than a waste of time, since it would unquestionably injure
your cause.

§ 61. *Additional Suggestions.* — Re-examination arises
from a right to explain.   It is often so advantageous that a
case may be won by its judicious exercise, while it is usually
so innocent of evil that it would require the utmost ingenuity of the most experienced counsel to make it the means of
losing one.   You must have a thorough knowledge of your
facts, and have watched every question of the cross-examination with the utmost vigilance, to take the full benefit of your
right, and to make your case stand out in the bolder relief
which the cross-examination will afford to it.   But nothing
is more tedious, or more irritating to judge or jury, than to
see an advocate floundering in re-examination among facts
which he only displaces and confuses, thinking he must
needs ask something because there has been a long, and it
may be, severe cross-examination.   First *ascertain what
fact has been displaced or obscured,* and *what new matter
introduced,* and then you will know what requires to be re-
arranged and what to be explained, before you rise to put a
single question.

In re-examination, as in cross-examination, after learning
thoroughly how to do it, the next branch of learning to
which the student had best direct his assiduous attention
is —*How not to do it!*

CHAPTER VI.—THE REPLY.

The reply is always of great importance, and a struggle is frequently made for the "last word." Many persons affect to disbelieve in it, but certainly not those who are able by their eloquence to avail themselves fully of its advantages. Even evidence itself is sometimes sacrificed for the sake of the reply, although I am not sure that if the evidence be of the smallest value, this is a course which ought to be pursued. However powerful arguments may be, facts are more powerful still. Nevertheless, it is frequently a question, whether the advocate will reply on his address for the verdict, or call witnesses and give the reply to his opponent. Under any circumstances, however — except in a case where one advocate is powerful and the other weak of speech — the reply is a valuable privilege. Some-

speeches doubtless are worse than none at all, and may even
assist the other side by means of contrast.

§ 62. *Endeavor to Secure the Judge.*—No one will doubt,
I presume, that the first thing to do is to secure the attention of the jury. The next, that of the judge. Although
I call this second, it is very often of the first importance, as
frequently, when you have not the jury with you, you may
win by having the judge. He is always a powerful advocate to follow on your side; therefore gain his attention if
you can. I heard not long ago a defeated advocate say to
his successful opponent: " The judge got you the verdict."
" Yes," replied the latter, " but I got the judge." If he
takes your view of law and facts, the verdict follows either
there or elsewhere. He will, however, take at times a somewhat different view from yours, both of the facts and the
law; and then, in spite of opposition, you must endeavor to
win your way to the jury. This is the object of the reply
as of the other processes of the case. And how to accomplish it is a question, on the consideration of which too
much time and study cannot well be bestowed.

§ 63. *Advocacy is Speaking.* — The hints here given —
based upon observation and experience — may be useful,
although no number of " hints " of themselves will ever
make an advocate. The art of speaking, logical reasoning
and rhetoric, are all involved in this branch of an advocate's
duty. It must, however, be assumed that the reader has
made these the subject of considerable study. If he have
not, he had better turn his attention to them without delay
and with the most assiduous care. The art of speaking, I
am quite sure, is by no means cultivated as it should be, and
a ridiculous fashion has sprung up of late years of under-
valuing it as a means of advocacy. The fact, however,
remains, that the best speaker is still the most successful
advocate as a rule; and if a man is to make anything either
of himself or his case by addressing a jury, the more perfectly he can speak, the better it will be for both. No pains
or labor should be spared upon this branch of an advocate's

duty. To speak well is to succeed, and the better you can
speak, the fewer competitors you will find in the field
against you.

§ 64. *Do not Flatter the Jury.*—In conciliating a jury
so as to put them on good terms with you and secure their
attention, you should be careful, as I have before observed,
not to adopt a practice too common with young advocates,
namely, that of flattering them. You must not forget that
their nature is by no means changed because they are in the
jury-box. "*Stroking*" a jury is not a dignified proceeding; talking about their intelligence, as though it were
necessary to remind them that they are not altogether
fools, is the worst means to make them believe in your intelligence or knowledge of mankind.

Again, obtruding upon them the information that they
are *sensible* men, will not improve their opinion of you or
interest them in any way. What you have to do is not to
convince them that *they* are sensible, but—that *you* are!
Nor is it necessary to remind them that you are " quite certain that they will take an honest and impartial view of the
facts:" this is not replying, nor is it rhetoric; it is the
flimsiest of claptrap. Hackneyed expressions are always
ineffective, stale and irritating; they show a poverty of
idea as well as language, and exhibit the weakest style of
advocacy. There is no necessity to argue with the jury
upon their honesty, as though there were some doubt about
it; or their impartiality, as if you had a suspicion that they
were being influenced by a strong interest on the other side..
You must not let the jury imagine that you are attempting
to humbug them. Any observations will be simply foolish,.
that have for their object the inducing the jury to believe in
themselves; a far better attempt will be to make them believe in *you!* " If," says Whately, " the pleader can induce a jury to believe not only in his own general integrity
of character, but also in his sincere conviction of the justice
of his client's cause, this will give great additional weight.
to his pleading, since he will thus be regarded as a sort of

witness in the cause. And this accordingly is aimed at, and often with success, by practiced advocates. They employ the language and assume the manner of full belief and strong feeling."

§ 65. *Nor Attack your Opponent.*—Another bad way of beginning a reply is to attack your opponent or his associates, or the client. The jury care for none of them. You have to demolish the case of your opponent, not *him*. Besides abuse is neither argument nor advocacy; and any personal attack is mere abuse, except when it is used to denounce a witness whose evidence requires to be so dealt with. Junius says in one of his letters: "The choice at least announced to us a man of superior capacity and knowledge. Whether he be so or not, let his dispatches, as far as they have appeared—let his measures, as far as they have operated—determine for him. In the former we have seen strong assertions without proof, declamation without argument, and violent censures without dignity or moderation, but neither correctness in the composition nor judgment in the design."

§ 66. *Nor Notice his Attacks.*—Nor will it assist your case to answer any attacks which your opponent may foolishly have made upon you. Avoid being drawn from legitimate argument into a personal encounter. The dispute is not yours, but your client's, and it is extremely selfish to indulge in a personal conflict at his expense. If anything has been said which required an answer from you, the time for giving it was at the moment of its utterance. When you reply, it is not *your* case, but that of your client that demands the undivided attention of the jury.

Securing this attention is as much due to the manner in which you address your hearers as the substance of what you say. The most thorough earnestness is the all-important quality either to possess or to assume. A quiet colloquial sentence or two, with not too much of solemnity, uttered as if you had the fullest confidence in them without telling them so, and as if you also had the fullest confidence in yourself, without asserting it, will be pretty sure to establish a good understanding between you and the jury at the commencement. If you can not succeed in this, your address will have little effect, however powerful ; whereas, if you do succeed, every argument will have weight in proportion to its relevancy to the issue.

§ 67. *Order and Arrangement.*—The next thing to be attended to now, although it was the first thing to prepare before you rose, is the order and arrangement of your speech. No address can be good without this, and it can not be altogether bad with it. The minds of your hearers will more easily follow and appreciate when you take them along the order of circumstances as they occurred, or, as I would say, the main road, than if you led them a steeple-chase across the country. You should so arrange the arguments that they can see what is to follow as you advance along the line of facts, and it will appear as if it must be correct, because the one fact follows so naturally upon another. The mind better understands a map of a country where the counties are plainly marked, than where the boundaries are undefined. The whole case is spread out before the jury like a map, and the better its divisions are traced the more fully will their relative bearings be understood. This will be the result of a due order and arrangement of your speech. Your opponent has made his comments upon the case ; has put prominently forward his own facts, and placed yours as far as possible in the shade ; has damaged some, and demolished others. You must now not only perform a like process with regard to his, but must throw light into the dark places, and draw out your own facts from their temporary obscurity.

Observation has taught me that the best advocates (who invariably proceed by system), as a general rule, adopt the course of grappling with their opponent's case first. It is fresh in the minds of the jury, and the best time to deal with it is before it has been long enough there to make a deep impression. If you return to it after dealing with your own case, you attack it instead of removing it, and may leave it still the last and deepest impression.

§ 68. *Avoid Minute Criticism.*—In doing this, care must be taken to *avoid dwelling on minor discrepancies in your opponent's evidence, or upon the trivialities of the case.* Minute criticisms impair the force of your address like grains of dust in the wheels of machinery. They produce friction, and retard instead of advancing your cause. The jury are apt to think you have nothing better to urge, and when you come to greater matters will be jaded and wearied, and a good deal of the effect of your speech will be lost. You can not assign any position in which trivial criticism should be placed, and the probability is, therefore, that it will be out of place anywhere. If you attempt it before coming to your main argument the jury will be wearied, and if after, your arguments will lose some of their force. Besides this, you endow trifles with a fictitious importance. You place them before the jury and magnify them as though you brought them under a lens. Whately says: "Too earnest and elaborate a refutation of arguments which are really insignificant. or which their opponent wishes to represent as such, will frequently have the effect of giving them importance. Whatever is slightly noticed and afterwards passed by with contempt, many readers and hearers will very often conclude (sometimes for no better reason) to be really contemptible. But if they are assured of this again and again with great earnestness, they often begin to doubt it."

§ 69. *Effect of Testimony.*—It should also be borne in mind in replying, that what you have really to deal with is *not the testimony* of the witnesses. but the *effect* of it, or the real *evidence* to which it is reduced by the process of examination. As an illustration of this distinction, I may mention a case tried some time since by Mr. Justice (now Lord Justice) Brett. The action was brought by the owner of a valuable horse, against a farrier, for negligence, by improperly shoeing; in consequence whereof the horse fell lame and had to be killed. The plaintiff endeavored to prove that the hind shoes of horses were, to use a familiar expression, "rights and lefts." The defendant swore that this was a totally erroneous supposition. His witnesses testified to the same effect. Perjury was not attributed to any of them. They seemed to believe their own testimony, and the plaintiff was not prepared with evidence to the contrary, as the point arose during the trial from an examination of the shoe by the counsel, who placed it in the hands of the defendant, and asked whether it was not made for the near foot. The witness said it would do for either the near or off foot. He was then pressed as to whether he would put it on either the one or the other, as it might chance. He answered "yes." The nails were now placed through the holes, which, being properly beveled, gave to their points on the one limb of the shoe an outward direction, and on the other side a different inclination. The defendant was asked, whether looking at that fact, he was prepared to say the shoe was not made for the near foot. He said it was not. He was then asked how it was that the nails in the two sides pointed at different angles? Answer: "It was the fashion." The Judge: "The fashion with all farriers?" Answer: "Yes." In summing up, the learned judge (taking the testimony of the witnesses, and judging it, not by its truth but from its effect), said: "If you find a general mode of doing a particular thing, you may depend upon it, there is some good reason for so doing it, especially where it obtains universally in some mechanical business. If all farriers make horse-shoes with beveled holes slanting in one direction on one side, and in another direction on the other, you may be sure that is not done from mere caprice. What is the effect of the testimony? It is to show that if the shoe on which the nails slant in a particular direction be placed on the off-foot, they will come out through the hoof and enable the farrier to clench them ; but if the shoe be fixed on to the near foot, they will have a tendency to penetrate the frog of the foot, and so cause

pain and lameness to the animal. The question is, was that
the case here? Was a shoe, intended for the off-foot, fastened
to the near one?''   The jury came to the conclusion that
that had been the case from the effect of the evidence; the
testimony, uncontradicted, being directly to the contrary.

If you can deal with the effect of the evidence instead of
with the truthfulness of a witness, I need hardly say it will
be so much the better for your case; so, if instead of attacking the credibility of a witness, you dispute his accuracy, his memory or judgment.   "Men are apt," says
Whately, "to judge amiss of situations, persons and circumstances, concerning which they have no exact knowledge,
by applying to these the measure of their own feelings and
experience, the result of which is that a correct account of
these will often appear to them unnatural, and an erroneous
one natural.''   Juries never like to believe that a witness
has committed perjury, especially if he have no interest in
the case.   Nor does it please them to hear character assailed. If you fall foul of the jury in these respects, you
may as well sit down for all the good you can do your
client.

The *effect of the testimony*, then, is what you have to deal
with in reply.   But if it becomes necessary, as it sometimes
must, to ask the jury to disbelieve a witness, and you can
put it on no easier ground than that he is untruthful, you
should avoid doing it by denunciation; that is only to be
used in extreme cases, where virtuous indignation will do
some mischief to the inner man if pent-up longer; but you
will find " half steam up," as a friend of mine calls it, will
carry you along quite fast enough in any event. Your just
indignation should only be sufficiently let off, that it may
communicate itself to the pent-up indignation of the jury,
and let that off with it in the shape of a verdict.   The best
way of asking a jury to disbelieve an opponent's witness is
to call attention to the evidence of one or two of your own.
Some matters will depend partly upon the facts and partly
upon the witness's judgment or understanding of those

facts to which he speaks; his view may be entirely wrong, and his conclusion, which he puts forward as a fact, wrong also. I again have recourse to Whately, who confirms me upon this point. "If," he says, "a person states he saw in the East Indies a number of persons who had been sleeping exposed to the moon's rays, afflicted with certain symtpoms, and that after taking a certain medicine they recovered, he is bearing testimony as to simple matters of fact; but if he declares that the patients were so affected in consequence of the moon's rays — that such is the general effect of them in that climate, his testimony, however worthy of credit, is borne to a different kind of conclusion, namely, not an individual but a general conclusion, and one which will rest not solely on the veracity, but also on the judgment of the witness." "Even in the other case, however, when the question relates to what is strictly a matter of fact, the intellectual character of the witness is not to be wholly left out of the account. A man may be strongly influenced by prejudice — to which the weakest men are ever the most liable — may even fancy he sees what he does not."

Intellectual character and capacity ought always to be taken into account, whenever the question involves intelligence above the commonest understanding. Positiveness generally increases in proportion to the ignorance of the witness. An ignorant person might swear the sun goes around the earth, merely because it seems to. That, no doubt, is an extreme mode of putting it; but very common instances of persons swearing to what seems to be, and mistaking it for what is, might be given, if they did not readily suggest themselves to the mind of the reader.

"*Le vrai n'est pas toujours le vraisemblable,*" is an adage worth remembering in reply. It is worth conveying to the minds of the jury, for they are very apt to judge by appearances themselves, and they are never better pleased than when enjoying the surprise of having been deceived by some appearance. They experience the sensation of having been told the answer to a riddle which they were unable to guess. If you can awaken that sensation, you will be pretty sure of your verdict.

§ 70. *Probabilities and Possibilities.*— Probabilities are of more value than possibilities. Juries, like other people, attach more weight to them. They are extremely valuable in reply, and should be made the most of. Opportunities which the witnesses had of seeing or knowing that which they depose to is also a matter of the highest moment. The means of forming a judgment is another, and all these may be used with a jury in short and terse argument for the purpose of obtaining an adverse opinion to the evidence, without the necessity of asking them to say it is perjured. Exhaust all argument before you come to that, unless you know that perjury has been committed, and then come to it boldly and at once, without giving the perjurer an opportunity of escape. You will have observed that you have left for a moment, but for a moment only, the line marked out, of dealing with your opponent's case before presenting your own. But it is necessary in order to contrast the evidence, and will materially assist you in dealing with that of your opponent. It will not interfere with the course of your argument, but will be advantageous to it when you come to review the facts of your own case.

It need scarcely be said that in examining the opposing evidence you will not fail to remark the points of contradiction, or any important variance in the versions of the different witnesses, or neglect to point out the improbabilities of the theory advanced on the other side, or to show that the case does not cover the ground occupied by your own.

§ 71. *Presenting your own Testimony.*— Having gone through the material witnesses and disposed of them as far as possible, or left them to be routed by-and-by, the next duty will be to bring your own evidence to the front and once more present your case to the jury. You may now collate your testimony as given by the several witnesses, and show the case in its completeness and consistency.

At all times you should be concise, but especially at this
stage, and as short as may be. If you are not a good
speaker, it will be better to be brief, because indifferent
speaking does not tell very much; if you are a good speaker,
because good speaking tells a good deal. A good speech,
however short, goes all the way; but the stretch of mere
windy talk invariably stops short of its object. But even a
good speaker should guard against smothering his points
with too many words; the most fluent advocates require
most pruning at the commencement. All you want is to so
place your facts that they will stand out boldly defined, like
fruit upon a wall-tree where there is not too much wood.
Almost a barrenness of language, rather than an exuberance,
will be beneficial. You must avoid clothing a fact with the
drapery of fine language, and also the making too many
points at once. Do not present them like a bunch of grapes,
or half of them will be unseen. Let each be made distinctly
and separately, as though it were a work of art, and made
for the jury's critical examination; and when once made,
let it alone.

Having thus presented your points in detail and made the
best exhibition of them separately, you may now marshal
them together and bring them up once for all in a body.
To use a military phrase, which doubtless most of my
readers will understand, you may have a " march past " to
conclude with, and that, to my judgment, is a most effective
mode of showing the strength and equipment of your
forces.

§ 72. *Avoid Common-Place Sayings.*—There is a matter
which, but for its constant recurrence, I should not think it
necessary to mention, and that is, that conventional phrases
should, as a rule, be avoided; so should stale adages, which
from common use become only one remove from slang itself; they show a poverty of ideas and a lack of originality,
besides enfeebling your address. A man does not do himself justice when he has recourse to a common-place saying
for the purpose of illustrating a point. It is neither orna-

mental nor argumentative, and is more adapted to the Peep-show than the Forum. But the great danger attending common-places, is that they are so feeble and so easily demolished. What is the use of "Gentlemen, there is an old saying that good wine needs no bush," etc., etc., against a speaker who follows with sound logical argument; or if it be a matter of pure inference, who meets such rubbish with the strong and forcible language of common sense? The "old saying" may provoke a laugh, but the new say-ing is the one that will make the impression.

§ 73. *Illustration when Proper.*— Not that illustrations are to be ignored; they are among the most useful of all the means employed by the rhetorician. They bring home your meaning with a force and power that nothing can sur-pass; but the illustration, if nothing else, should be original. It should be a flash from your own mind, not a mere reflec-tion of some one else's lantern, however brilliantly it may burn. Whately says : "There is very little, comparatively, of energy produced by any metaphor or simile that is in common use, and already familiar to the hearer." An illustration, however homely, if original and apt, is always pleasing and forcible.

§ 74. *Avoid Emotion.*— I have already advised the ad-vocate against a too liberal exhibition of emotion. It need scarcely be added, that appealing to the passions of a jury in reply in a direct manner is out of place and unfair. They are not to determine by passion or feeling, and attempts to rouse the emotions may mislead the judgment. The sym-pathies of the jury are a proper subject to reach, if you can do it by the facts and not by meretricious sentiment; this is a legitimate exercise of the art of advocacy and of the powers of eloquence; and the art consists in so presenting the facts, that they will accomplish that which you are for-bidden to attempt. But it would be presumptuous in me to discuss those higher gifts of the orator, which can never be learnt or acquired. All I intend to say is, that any attempt to influence a jury by an appeal to their feelings, is certain to meet with reprobation. It is clumsy and coarse at the best, and as bad as an open act of intimidation; if you can not reach their sympathies without a violent attack, you had better rest upon your facts, and reserve your pathos for your client.

§ 75. *Do not Introduce Prejudice.*— Nor will you ever succeed in getting the judge with you, if you openly attempt to introduce prejudice. It is a kind of rhetorical burglary, which none but those who can not effect their object by other means would ever perpetrate. It is logically wrong as well as morally. If the circumstances are such as naturally excite the sympathies of the jury in favor of your client, you have no need to make a flourish of trumpets to announce the fact; if they are not such, you will fail to move them by the employment of feeble arts for that purpose; besides which, you will probably set the judge against you, if not against your case; for you may be sure that in his desire to do justice between the parties, he will do his best to prevent your winning by unfair means; if it unhappily follow that you lose a good case by his endeavor to defeat an unfair attempt to win it, the fault will not be his, but yours.

§ 76. *The Elements of a Good Reply.*—A reply should be comprehensive and compact; it should be temperate, as well as bold. In its moderation will be its strength. Violence of language is invariably weak; loudness of tone, but a noisy accompaniment at the best, which stuns the ear instead of making the speaker heard. With a tone always above the natural key there can be no modulation, which I take to be the music of oratory; the effect of which is to entertain while the feast of reason proceeds.

Lord Brougham said of Erskine: "Juries have declared that they felt it impossible to remove their looks from him when he had riveted, and as it were, fascinated them by his first glance. Then hear his voice of surpassing sweetness, clear, flexible, though exquisitely fitted to strains of earnestness." "His action," says Espinasse, "was always ap-

propriate, chaste, easy, natural.   *   *   *   The tones of
his voice, though sharp, were full, destitute of any tinge of
Scotch accent, and adequate to any emergency—*almost scientifically modulated to the occasion.*" Speaking of action,
I may say, that all the advice ever given by would-be
teachers of the art of speaking, as to gesture, is absolutely
worthless. A good speaker has a natural and appropriate
gesture ; a bad speaker has none at all. You can no more
learn to gesture, than you can learn to be handsome.

§ 77. *Do not Exaggerate.*—" Whatever you exaggerate,
you weaken," said the present Solicitor-General in consultation a short time since ; a maxim worth remembering,
both in opening a case and replying. You may overdo
your own facts, or say too much against those of your opponent ; and it is a good thing at the bar, as soon as you
can do so, to " let your moderation be known unto all
men." And moderation in voice is no less pleasing than in
language. I have heard some men shout so in reply, that
you would have thought the jury some poor shipwrecked
wretches on a rock, while one from shore was trying to
make himself heard above the tempest, and I have wondered what the feelings of the shipwrecked ones must be as
they listened to this thundering Genius of the storm.

§ 78. *The Peroration.* — A word as to the Peroration,
which should not, like the end of a squib, be all bang, nor
like the finish of a rocket, all stars above every one's head ;
but it should be a common-sense and pleasant finish — attractive, impressive and as polished as may be. It should
leave upon the mind a pleasing recollection. It should be
well construed, appropriate and short. As the exordium is
intended, with a few well chosen words, to secure the
hearer's attention, so the peroration is designed to leave
upon his mind the satisfaction that his attention has been
well bestowed. One or two instances of well turned
forensic perorations by eminent advocates, I have selected
as examples of conciseness, brevity and beauty, which will
be found in another chapter.

§ 79. *Lord Brougham on the Duty of an Advocate.*— I.
have thought it right to conclude this subject by referring
to the extraordinary language used by Lord Brougham in a.
very celebrated case, which, I believe, has misled a great
many more, to the danger of their unfortunate clients as·
well as the peril of their own prospects. The young are too·
apt to believe what a great man says, especially if he be an
authority in the profession they follow. Great men often.
utter small sayings, which would not be listened to if ordi--
nary men said them, and nothing is more foolish than to
take even a wise man's sayings without examining them for·
ourselves. It is not because a great or a wise man says a
thing that we are to implicitly believe and blindly follow it;.
and I take leave to say that an honorable man, if he thinks
seriously, must disagree with the following proposition of
Lord Brougham, who was certainly impetuous, however·
great :

"There are many whom it may be needful to remind, that an advo--
cate — by the sacred duty of his connection with his client — knows, in·
the discharge of that office, but one person in the world—that client and.
none other. To serve that client by all expedient means; to protect
that client at all hazards and costs to all others (even the party already
injured), and, amongst others, to himself, is the highest and most unquestioned of his duties. And he must not regard the alarm, the suffering, the torment, the destruction, which he may bring upon any others..
Nay, separating even the duties of a patriot from those of an advocate,.
he must go on, reckless of the consequences, if his fate should unhappily be to involve his country in confusion for his client."

Although some portion of this sweeping proposition
might be assented to, and especially in the circumstances
which called them forth, there is surely much that an hon--
orable man would shrink from even though he give full.
scope to the meaning of the word " expedient." In the·
impetuosity of advocacy, such as Brougham was stirred up·
by the occasion to employ, it might have been excusable to·
use such language; but if it be examined, its propositions·
can scarcely be assented to.

§ 80. *Criticism on his Words.*— An advocate can hardly
claim a higher privilege than his client could claim for himself, were he defending his own cause. Would he be permitted to disregard the suffering, the torment, the destruction which he might bring upon others? And under what
circumstances could the expediency of bringing down such
overwhelming calamities arise? If it could never be expedient, all the rest of the sentence, with its catalogue of
evils, might have been left out. If it could be expedient,
when?

Assume a witness to have been thirty years ago sen-
tenced to transportation; that he had become since a flour-
ishing merchant in England; was surrounded with a family,
and enjoyed the society of many friends, to all of whom
the history of his early life was happily unknown. He
comes into the witness-box to depose to some fact material
to the issue, and gives his evidence. Would it be tolerated
that counsel should ask if thirty years ago he was trans-
ported? But suppose the counsel thought it " expedient "
to bring it out. I presume he is to be the sole judge of the
expediency. What would follow? The ruin, perhaps, of
the witness, the shame of his friends, and the misery of his
family! No one else on earth is to be considered but the
client who is bringing his action, it may be on a paltry bill
of exchange. It seems to me that such a course of advocacy would be cruel and unjustifiable.

An advocate should be tender of the feelings of others,
although engaged in the " sacred service " of his client;
and above all things he ought to be the guardian and not the
destroyer of private character; he should observe the
golden rule of " doing unto others as he would be done
by," nor should he lose or suspend the feelings of a Chris-
tian and a gentleman; he should regard " the alarm, the
suffering, the torment, the destruction which he may bring
upon others;" " to serve his client " may be " his highest
duty as on advocate," but it is yet hoped it will not cause

him to forget his duties as a man, or prevent him from throwing up his brief rather than do a dishonorable action. Besides this, an advocate who casts destruction broadcast may involve his client in the general ruin, and is sure in any event to injure him in the estimation of the jury.

CHAPTER VII.—Opening and Closing Defendant's Case.

Opening the defendant's case is a matter of great importance, and differs materially in its method from that of opening the case for the plaintiff.

In the latter, the path is generally clear; in the former, there is every obstacle that the circumstances of the case or the ingenuity of your opponent can interpose.

§ 81. *A Hopeless Case.*—If ever a case looks hopeless, it should be your own at this moment. The jury, if they had to determine the case now, should be unanimous in favor of your opponent. If the facts are not strong, however, or the counsel is not strong, or has not made the most of his case, the jury will be divided, but none of them, as I once heard a juryman say, "very unanimous" in the plaintiff's favor. In these circumstances your verdict is as good as won. Disaster awaits the advocate who has not the jury with him at this stage of the case.

In a season of such depression you will often find an extraordinary accession of good feeling take possession of his breast.

Wouldn't it be better for all parties to agree, and for an amicable arrangement to be come to? If the defendant's counsel be wise, he will yield to no such blandishments. The flag of truce is but the signal of distress, and he should push on his advantages to their legitimate conclusion.

I once heard a defendant's counsel say, in circumstances like these, when his opponent asked if he could suggest any course :—

"Yes," said he, "I can—a verdict for the defendant."

You should not capitulate when you have won the battle, or surrender when the enemy is in full retreat. I have seen a good many do this without knowing it. It is not, however, invariably the fact that a weak case for the plaintiff is at its strongest at the close. I have frequently seen the defendant's counsel strengthen it materially. I have also seen the cross-examination of his own witnesses *absolutely prove it*.

It follows, therefore, that very great discretion and skill are requisite in opening the case for the defendant. It is surrounded with obstacles, and it is a far more difficult task, than opening that for the plaintiff.

§ 82. *Where to Attack.* — The first thing to decide is at what point to commence the attack. A good deal may depend upon this. You may expend much energy in fruitless work. The weak places are undoubtedly attractive, but as a rule, should be reserved, because at a later period the effect will be greater and the demolition *appear* to be more complete. Attack, therefore, the strong points first, but not by direct blows. You cannot knock down a substantial wall by butting your head against it. There are improbabilities and inconsistencies, perhaps, or partialities to deal with. You may possibly get at these, and shake the very foundations on which the whole fabric rests.

If you have accomplished anything by cross-examinations, it will be of inestimable service at this period of the case. But your speech must be directed first to weaken

before you bring to bear the reserved forces which you have
stored up as the result of your cross-examination.

§ 83. *How to Attack.*— That which was to be avoided in
opening a case for the plaintiff is the strength of the defendant's opening—namely, argument. I do not mean to
affirm that you can demolish an isolated fact by argument;
but a series of facts, some of which may be true and some
false, may be made to demolish one another. You may
always make the lean kine devour the fat, and one cadaver-
ous-looking fact has been known to swallow up even the
substance of an honest case. If you can show that, assuming all the facts to be true, they do not *necessarily* prove
the plaintiff's case, you will have gone a long way to establish your own.

By this mode of proceeding you will have already dealt
with the strongest portions of the case against you. When
you arrive at the weaker parts, avoid, above all things, a
furious and vehement onslaught; otherwise they will appear
more formidable than they really are. You scarcely want
a sledge-hammer to drive home a tin-tack. Let the force
be proportioned to the task. A well-worded argument will
be infinitely more effective than fiery declamation, which
often reminds me of the process of hiving a new swarm of
bees, namely, an incessant beating on a hollow pan.

By removing some of your opponent's points in a quiet
but effective manner, the jury will believe you must be
right with regard to many others that you have not removed.
You will gain credit for a great deal more than you have
actually accomplished, and your success will have a retrospective effect. In other words, the more respectable facts
will get a bad character by being found in company with
those which you prove to be weak and corrupt. Associa-
tion, whether of ideas, facts or people, has a great influence on spectators, even as the surroundings of our life
impress it for good or evil, for happiness or misery.

It often happens that a witness is called for the plaintiff, whose evidence is worthless. It may not be valueless to you. But by no means be over eager to attack him. He is like a short man in a crowd ; and if you want to make use of him don't tread him down, but carefully *hold him up.* Keep him as a surprise for the end of your comments on the plaintiff's witnesses, and then hold him up above the crowd and make him the principal figure in the group. Whatever he has said in your favor will, of course, materially assist and confirm your argument. You will, in fact, be proving your case by the opponent's witnesses —a happy mode of conducting a cause to a successful conclusion, when you are permitted to do so. An admission against the party making it possesses a force which belongs to no other class of evidence except documentary.

§ 84. *Speeches and — Speeches.*—A bad speech will impoverish the best of cases. It is like dressing a millionaire in rags. Your case will in all probability be judged by the speech with which it is introduced, and first impressions are not easily removed. A bad speech hoists the flag of distress at the outset, and although he may excite a good deal of commiseration, no one will come to his rescue.

On the other hand, I have seen many a case won by the opening speech for the defendant. Everything seemed to be swept away before it, and a clear field left for the evidence that was to follow. And it may be said, if once the defendant's counsel gets a thorough hold upon the jury in his opening speech, the case is as good as won. The evidence will appear to be merely supplementary, to confirm the jury in the opinion they will have formed. It is true, facts are more powerful than argument, but when argument and eloquence lay hold of a fact that is not absolutely sound, they will press it out of all recognition, and dispose of it as though it were a bubble.

There is scarcely any subject which men study less, and know so little about as speaking. There is nothing they can not measure more accurately than its influence on the human mind. The best case may be ruined by a bad speech,

:as a splendid fortune may be thrown away by a fool; while a good speech will impart, or appear to impart, to a bad case, something of its own excellencies.   There is nothing of art in the speeches of ordinary advocates; but where it is judiciously employed against an advocate who has none, the result will scarcely be doubtful, other chances being equal. It is a breech-loader to a pop-gun.

§ 85. *The Reply must be Borne in Mind.*—The fact of a reply looming in the distance, should always be borne in mind.   You must anticipate it at every step, and so shape your own arguments, that they will receive as little damage as possible from the approaching simoon.   A fallacious argument is bad enough, but it sometimes wins; a false one is dangerous and generally fatal.   It will place you in the position of being detected in an act of deception.   So will opening a piece of evidence that you cannot prove, or asserting that something has not been proved which in reality has been.   These are blunders in advocacy which are constantly being made to the detriment of clients; not made from want of practice, but for lack of studying advocacy as an art.   Practice will not cure these errors.   The carpenter who makes a door too small may have made many doors, but his blunder comes from inaccurate measurement.   When you commence to address the jury, they will adjust themselves to the task of listening, as though they were about to be entertained with the second act of an amusing drama. They will readily yield you their attention, and be curious to know what answer you will make to all that has been urged on the other side.   I have seldom known them to make up their minds at this stage of the case.   They may or may not believe all the evidence; but whether they do or not, they will accord you a patient hearing.   But the curiosity of the jury may be quickly gratified.   You may lose their attention and your case by a few sentences, or by hobbling along as though you were doing penance for your client.

After a few unimportant but engaging sentences, a good

speaker will continue to stimulate the curiosity of his hearers by some remark which either wins their admiration or throws a flash of light upon some unobserved part of the case. Persistently exciting anew the attention is one of the great principles of the art of speaking. A new simile, an original remark, or a well turned period are all means to this end in a well conceived speech.

Having disposed of the weaker points of your opponent's case and attacked the strong ones by well arranged argument, the next duty will be to present your own facts, and in doing this the great rule to observe is *to arrange them with due regard to probabilities*. This is not always done; it is sometimes not even thought of. The same facts may be so ill arranged, that collateral circumstances (never to be lost sight of, although irrelevant as evidence) may raise the strongest improbabilities against you. On the other hand, by a skilful arrangement, the opposite effect will be produced.

§ 86. *Arrangement of Evidence.*— A great deal will depend upon an artistic arrangement of your evidence at this stage, so that it may not only stand out in the best light, but be so placed that its position may cast your opponent's as much as possible into the shade. As before observed, contrast plays a great part in advocacy. But mere naked contrast is not all that you can make of your facts, if they are in contradiction to those of your opponent. You will have but half learnt your art if you rest here. Contrast the opposing facts as forcibly as you can by all means, but so *place them that your own will appear to be the more natural when regarded in connection with surrounding circumstances.* If you place two young people of opposite sexes near a church door, it will look much more like a wedding than if you seat them in the stall of a theatre. And if you make the bells ring while they are coming from the church, the jury will undoubtedly believe they have just been married, though neither the church nor the bells would be evidence of the marriage.

When you have to deal with evidence which is eccentric, or absurdly exaggerated, you need not labor as though it were worthy of the gravest consideration — simply point out its grotesqueness, as though the matter were worthy of notice on that account only.

If a witness has sworn to something contrary to all human experience, you need not weary the jury by arguing that such evidence is unreliable. It is when you approach facts within the range of probability, and deposed to by trustworthy witnesses, that your powers of argument will be put to the test. Probabilities must here be relied upon, and the smallest circumstance will often prove of the greatest importance. The case will resemble a puzzle composed of a number of pieces which fit into one another. If there were duplicates of some which did not belong to it, you would examine the *edges*, the *color*, and the *grain of the wood*, in order to detect the true from the false. In like manner you must deal with the facts of your opponent's case, when they conflict with yours, and yet seem to fit in with surrounding circumstances.

But in whatever difficulties you may find yourself, there should be no distressful laboring. A ship makes little progress when she labors.

§ 87. *Not too much Recommendation.*—If your witnesses are respectable, you need not detract from their respectability by over proclaiming it. The jury will believe your witnesses to be ordinarily respectable, unless you take overmuch pains to convince them of it. It is only counterfeit character that, like counterfeit beauty, requires a good deal of touching up.

Where a good witness is cross-examined as to character, it is as good as vouched for by the other side.

If you saw a man being led down Fleet Street by another who kept shouting, " Here's an honest man ! Look at this honest man ! " you would suspect the pair of some roguish design upon your credulity. The worst recommendation a man can have is too much praise, and there is no worse advocacy than making a person impossibly good.

The next thing to observe is to introduce your evidence *with a view to effect.* " Of course, of course," I hear on all sides. But it is not of course. This, like a good many other hints, is as much needed by many experienced advocates as it is by juniors. Practice is not sufficient to perfect an advocate. Take an illustration (if not too humble), from a well arranged shop window, where many costly articles are exhibited. The arrangement is a matter of art and study ; mere practice would not produce its effect. It pleases, and you can scarcely know why. It is because no one thing offends the eye by obtruding itself upon your notice. The harmony produced by the artistic arrangement is such, that *the leading objects attract your attention without appearing to do so, and are set off by the surrounding articles.* There is no crowding, and everything is displayed. If you can as artistically arrange your evidence in your speech, you will produce an effect which will not be easily removed. The very " setting out " of your case may win it.

I will go one step further, and affirm that if the plaintiff have somewhat the better case, but yours be the better advocated, the chances will be immensely in your favor.

Avoid parenthesis as much as possible ; but if you employ one, let it be for the purpose of emphasis. It requires some skill (not so much the skill that comes from practice, as that which is produced by careful study) to do this effectively. If done well, your parenthesis will stand out like the principal object of a brilliant pyrotechnic display ; but if ill performed, it will be like a damp center-piece, which becomes a failure and the darkest spot of all.

§ 88. *All's Well that Ends Well.*—The best-worded sentence you can form should end your speech. A pleasant rhetorical flourish is always acceptable, while a well constructed peroration has many redeeming qualities. It will smooth over many a rugged point that has discovered itself

during the progress of your speech, and hearers often persuade themselves that it is a good address which *ends well.*
The jaded horse pricks up his ears at the end of a long
journey. Nor should it be forgotten that speaking does not
consist in mere words ; the effect produced on the mind by
a piece of real oratory *is a succession of images.* Men do
not *hear* a great speech so much as they *see* and *feel* it.
Hence it is that they weary of words which produce no
images. The child turning over a book without pictures is
exactly what an audience is to the mere spouter of words.

The orator is gifted with a magician's wand, which,
waved before his audience, produces scenes in which the
hearers are not merely spectators, but actors. Their sensa-
tious are quickened, so that they feel the influence of the
events brought before them, and participate in the joys and
sorrows by which they are surrounded.

I do not mean that a jury should be artificially or hyster-
ically excited, but that, by a proper employment of art, you
should cause them, not merely to hear what you say, but to
perceive the picture passing through your own mind, and to
be quickened with the impulse of your own sensations.

This is the art of opening the defendant's case. If
effectively performed, you need not fear the reply, although
you will utter no syllable without a thoughtful regard to it.

§ 89. *Summing Up.*—A few words will suffice as to summing up the defendant's case. Not that it is by any means
an unimportant branch of advocacy. On the contrary, it is
as invaluable as any privilege the advocate possesses. It
should be remembered that summing up your evidence is
not a repetition of the opening speech, in which you ana-
lyzed the plaintiff's evidence with sufficient skill to show
how worthless some of it was, and what residuum was left
to be disposed of by your own witnesses. If you performed
that duty half as well as I conceive you did, the parts that
you eliminated are gone forever. It only remained, therefore, to meet the matters that required answering with evidence on your part. You have now abundant scope for

your powers of reasoning, and for analytical comparison. There may be some opportunity, also, for something of declamation, of eloquence. and earnestness — it may be of *pathos* itself. But if so, remember it is the *pathos of facts* and the *eloquence of facts*, too, that you most need; if these fail, you might just as well beat a tambourine, and imagine you are an orchestra.

It is not absolutely forbidden to argue upon evidence antecedent to your own, although you have but the bare right to " sum up.'' The sum total may be not only your owr evidence, but your evidence supplemented in matter an. weight by the evidence of the plaintiff and his witnesses No rule can be laid down in this particular, nor will th judge be over strict in keeping you upon the direct line o your evidence.

§ 90. *Anticipate the Reply.*—As the reply will follov your speech, you will, of course, calculate what are the points likely to be made against you ; and if you have any knowledge of character at all, you will know what points have most impressed your adversary. Nearly all the cards having been played, you ought to know exactly what are left in your opponent's hand. You must, as a matter of course, strengthen those points which are likely to be assailed, and bring into strong prominence those portions of your case which are established beyond the reach of eloquence.

§ 91. *Keep a Good Look Out.*— If you have kept your eyes open, you will not be misled by any feint that may have been made by your opponent. If he has discovered a weakness in your case which you did not perceive, it will be little short of a calamity for your client when he comes to reply. This so often happens, that the greatest vigilance is necessary from the moment the case is launched till the last witness has been re-examined.

What word or remark of a witness may be the turningpoint in a case, you can never tell. What may be the test which the jury will apply to the evidence, you can but sur-

mise ; but that no word should escape your attention is as
certain as that, in surveying the ocean bed, no rock or prominence can be left unnoted with safety to the mariner.

One further observation I will make.   In summing up,
be sure you exhibit the qualities of a good arithmetician,
otherwise you may upset the calculations of your own witnesses.   The jury will tolerate no false casting up.   They
will require a correct total, whatever they may think of the
individual items.   Some they may disallow, others they
may admit, if your total be accurate ; if not, they may reject the whole with disgust, or even disappointment.

Bear also in mind that if you have two twos you need not
labor to convince the jury that the total is four ; and, above
all things, be careful that you do not attempt to prove that
it amounts to five.

CHAPTER VIII.—The Conduct of a Prosecution.

It may be well to give some hints with regard to this by no means unimportant branch of advocacy.

§ 92. *Let there be no Feeling.*—Let me say, then, first of all, that above everything it is important that an advocate should exhibit no feeling in the conduct of the prosecution. He is not the offended party, nor the minister of justice, as he is erroneously sometimes called. He is the presenter of the accused at the bar of justice, and is the last person who should exhibit emotion. Whoever the accused may be, and whoever the accuser, there should be but one unswerving desire on the part of the advocate, namely, to lay the facts of the case before the tribunal which is to judge of them. Neither the shocking nature of the crime, nor the heinous character of the accused, nor the exalted rank of the accuser, should disturb the mind or temper of the advocate.

But it is not in prosecutions for crimes of the deeper guilt that the danger of excited feeling has to be guarded against. It is in cases such as libel, where the circumstances may be particularly aggravated, and the accuser a person of distinguished position in society; or it may be in some other misdemeanor of the social sort, where mortal vindictiveness, rather than divine justice, seems occasionally to be the inspirer, if not the director of the proceedings.

But whatever may be the nature of the charge or the quality of accused or accuser, let there be no feeling — at least no manifestation of it. Nothing can be worse, either as a matter of abstract justice, or as a matter of mere advocacy. A man who throws feeling into a prosecution awakens an opposite sentiment in favor of the accused. The sense of fair play is outraged by any attempt to convict a man by declamation and angry expressions. Is he guilty? That is the question. You are not to denounce the crime; that has no doubt been committed by some one, and is none the deeper or the wickeder, denounce it as you will; you are not to denounce the man; he may not be guilty; and if not, shall the innocent be denounced? He may be guilty; what then? Are you his judge, or—his executioner? "Leave off from wrath before it be meddled with," in conducting a prosecution. I have known accused persons acquitted through too intense a desire to convict; especially in cases where self-constituted bodies of men support the public morality by public subscriptions.

§ 93. "*The Prisoner is Guilty.*"— The next thing to remember is, never to say that the prisoner is guilty. You have only to lay facts before the jury from which no other inference than that of guilt can reasonably arise. Guilty is the sum total of inferences and probabilities arising from the facts, and it is to be pronounced only by those who are sworn to try whether he be guilty or not guilty.

§ 94. *Do not Argue in Opening.*—Another error to avoid is argument at the opening of the case for the prosecution. At this stage there is nothing to argue (unless you want to argue that you are telling the truth), and its principal effect will be to throw doubt on your case. Facts that require nursing the moment they are presented, must be weak in-

deed; and you may depend upon it, such swaddling-clothes
will never keep life in them. What can be stronger or
healthier, than a plain statement of a simple fact?

Aye, but if it be not a simple fact, but a series of com-
pound facts, what then? It is a mere matter of arithmetic.
Reduce the compounds to simples; and for such analysis
there is no need for argument. The best opening of a case
for the prosecution is a clear and concise statement of facts,
without embellishment, without argument, and without feeling. It may be necessary to explain matters, or to separate
them, or to connect them, or to treat them in some other
manner by way of elucidation; but it is never necessary,
and is, therefore, bad advocacy to color them, or in any
way to alter their appearance, or to apply to them a far-
fetched, and possibly foreign meaning.

§ 95. *Exaggeration to be Avoided.*—Again, all exaggeration is to be avoided; you should neither magnify that
which you can prove, nor open a single fact that you cannot. It is not only bad as a matter of advocacy, but dishonest as a matter of morality. As the jury approaches
the evidence of the case by way of examination, the facts
should expand upon the view rather than diminish; as diminish they must, if you exaggerate them in your opening.
I have seen a jury shocked by the horrors of a charge in
the opening and smile upon the evidence in support of it,
and I have seen nothing left of the charge itself except the
frothy reply of the advocate, who seemed angry that a man
should be innocent. No art should be employed for the
mere purpose of convicting a prisoner, but there should be
no abandonment of it because a crime happens to be the
subject of your advocacy. It is your duty to convince the
jury of the guilt of the accused if you can do so fairly.
To accomplish this, you must present the facts in their natural order (which is art), and in the most comprehensive
manner (which is art), and in the most simple manner
(which also is art). But before all things, before even the
conviction of the guilty, it should be your care to refrain

from stating the smallest matter which in your conscience you do not believe to be capable of proof. If, inadvertently, this be done, as indeed it must sometimes from erroneous instructions, you should spare no pains to disabuse the minds of the jury of the impression which such a statement may have made. You can never tell what effect a word may have; a verdict may be influenced by the most trifling observation. For this reason you should instantly repair any mistake which may operate against the accused.

Another error, very frequently committed, should by all means be avoided. I mean that of telling a jury that you think you shall be able to prove so-and-so; or you think you shall be able to show so-and-so. This is unfair to the prisoner if you fail, and it is extremely weak if you succeed. What you know you can prove, open; what you are doubtful about, leave for the evidence.

§ 96. *Particular Expressions to be Avoided.* — Need it be said that expressions, such as " How on earth could the prisoner have known so-and-so?" and " How on earth could he have thought so-and-so?" should be avoided? And that language, such as "It is a lie! gentlemen," is not graceful or dignified. Nor should the counsel for the prosecution assume to himself the office of defending the prosecutor or prosecutrix, as the case may be. He may do so in the most efficient manner, if he be a skilful advocate; but that must not appear to be the main object of the prosecution.

With the clear understanding, then, that there is to be no struggle for a verdict, as though iniquitous vehemence were not unbecoming the " minister of justice," let us see what course of proceeding is best adapted to the object of the prosecution, namely, that of the ascertainment of the truth.

§ 97. *State the Charge Clearly.* — In the first place, the charge against the prisoner should be stated clearly and concisely; start not, my junior friend, it is not always stated clearly and concisely; nor is it always stated; and be not surprised when I say that it seldom is. The judge, generally, has to tell the jury, after all the speeches and all the evidence, what is the charge against him, and what is the nature of the charge. It has often struck me as remarkable, that young advocates, as a rule, both in prosecuting and defending, leave out the offense stated in the indictment. I have known many a man acquitted almost as soon as the nature of the charge has been stated upon the authority of the judge.

Now, there are many ways of stating a charge, but there is only one way to inform the minds of the jury of the offense which the accused is alleged to have committed. And the first necessary step is to strip it of the legal jargon in which it is enfolded. Since the days of Babel was no mortal language less " understanded" of the people than the lawyers' dialect; no man, however deep in linguistics, will ever be deep enough to get to the bottom of that unfathomable vortex.

But your duty is clear; you are the interpreter of this unknown thing to the people or " the country " before you. Wrapped as the simple matter is in the manifold incumbrances and technicalities of the law, how is a mortal common-sense jury to know whether the enfolded thing before them be a wolf or one's grandmother? But do not think you have made it intelligible, until you have reduced it to the poor phraseology of common sense; if it is ever necessary to call a spade a spade, it is among people who use it; and if " guilty knowledge " or "fraudulent intent" be the essence of the charge, you must not merely say so, but tell the jury in common parlance the legal meaning of the terms. Unless they understand the nature of the charge, they will never appreciate thoroughly the finer points of the evidence, which may be so important to lead them to a just conclusion. You need not, however, twaddle on to an unnecessary length, like a horse that is kept going by many bells with unmeaning music; you must learn to put the meaning of indictments into every-day language, and then you will reduce it to simplicity in a few words.

§ 98. *The Circumstances of the Case.* — You will next consider whether the condition, situation or circumstances of the prisoner be necessary to describe ; for be sure that whatever is unnecessary to be done in a prosecution should not be done. It may be that out of the circumstances of the accused springs the motive of the crime ; if so, probabilities spring, too, from the same root, and that is important to bring before the jury at the earliest moment. From his position, opportunity may be given ; if so, there is probability growing up and strengthened. From the situation of the accused, temptation — fatalest enemy — may be discovered. The crime first, therefore—the position of the accused next ; in other words, *crime, motive, opportunity.*

§ 99. — *The Facts of the Case.* — Now come the facts ; but be it remembered that nothing is to be stated, remote or near, that has not a direct bearing upon the issue. Everything that may prejudice the jury—as you love an easy conscience, and value your own character for honesty — must be carefully excluded ; and above all things avoid doing in an oblique manner that which it would be unfair to do directly. Nor is this warning unnecessary ; I have seen many err inadvertently in their zeal for the administration of justice, who, in a matter of private and social concern, would guard themselves from the faintest appearance of unfairness.

And now, let me again say *"order and arrangement,"* if you wish the jury thoroughly to understand the statement you have to make ; as you open your case, so should the witness be called to prove it ; the continuity of circumstances must not be broken, although there may be divers branches of the subject ; there may be many chapters, but they were enacted in order in the real history you are unfolding. If you want a model, go to the trial of Castro for perjury ; observe its chapters, its situations, its development.

You will sometimes find that the depositions are confused and complicated. Before the magistrates, where evidence is taken in portions, as it is obtained, and in the course of many adjournments or remands, it is next to impossible to follow any rule in this respect. But it will be your duty to separate and arrange the various portions of evidence before presenting them to the jury.

§ 100. *Trying to Prove too Much.*—It is extremely important that you should not allege too much, or you may in consequence prove too little. Nor is it a small matter that you should attempt to prove more than you can. Better succeed in reaching a moderate height, than fail in grasping what is beyond your compass. Every failure produces disappointment. It disappoints expectation and detracts from the merits of the case, if not from the merits of the counsel.

" Overlaying the case," as it is called, is a dangerous proceeding. A number of witnesses can not agree on all points ; I do not mean in words, because that would at once damn their evidence, but I mean as to facts themselves ; and if you call a number of witnesses, the chances are that you will call a number of contradictions ; and the moment you get one witness to contradict another upon any point how little material soever, if it be material, the jury, as a rule, will determine that portion of the evidence in favor of the accused, unless other circumstances lead them to a different conclusion. You will have given him already the benefit of one doubt.

Then, again, among your multitude may creep in some one or two of a disreputable kind ; you may not know them, but your " learned friend," if he have any skill, will soon introduce them to you ; and if their character or evidence be "shaky," as it is called forensically, it will lower the average of the whole ; at all events, the merits of your case will sink with it. It requires a number of respectable witnesses to buoy up a case laden with one whose character renders him unworthy of belief.

It is just as well, perhaps, not to convict an innocent man, so there is no occasion for overmuch zeal. Justice i

not vindicated by the sacrifice of a victim, but by the condemnation of the guilty. She may be blind, but she would
much rather withhold the rod until you can assure her by
unimpeachable evidence that it will not fall on the innocent.
Be careful, therefore, not to try to vindicate her too much ;
in fact, in conducting a prosecution, do not try to vindicate
anything.

§ 101. *Police Testimony.*—One other matter there is to
be on one's guard against, and that is, being overdone by
police testimony. Very few policemen are really untruthful, I believe ; and very few would unnecessarily " pile on
the evidence " against a man ; but all are zealous, and zeal
is a force, as we all know, that will sometimes impel us beyond the boundary line of discretion. They require to be
kept with a steady and firm hand ; for much zeal on their
part, like too much anxiety on yours, is sure to operate
against what the prosecution invariably calls " the interests
of public justice."

§ 102. *Anticipating the Defense.* — In proceeding with
your statement, there is often a danger of being led into an
anticipation of the defense that will be set up either to the
whole or to any portion of it. This ought never in a prosecution to be yielded to—if for no other reason, at least for
the very obvious one that if the prisoner be defended, you
have the right either of summing up or of replying. Such
expressions as, " It may be said by my learned friend,"
etc., etc., are not legitimately a part of an opening statement. But it is by no means improper, in favor of the
accused to present that view of a fact, which you find yourself obliged to deal with and dispose of. The moment you
show yourself eager to convict, the jury will suspect you
or the prosecutor of vindictive feeling, one of the worst
symptoms to manifest itself either at the bar or in the witness-box.

§ 103. *The Usual Defenses.*— There are two answers
only to a charge—one in law, the other in fact. These resolve themselves in practice to three :—1. The prisoner is

not the man (mistaken identity); 2. No intention to commit the act; or, 3. The act was never committed. I am speaking now of the nature of crimes and misdemeanors generally with which advocates have to deal at Assizes or Quarter Sessions; but I am not certain that I should not be perfectly accurate, if I applied the statement to the whole of the offenses in the statute book and at common law.

It is under one or other of these heads that the various "defenses" will range themselves. Insanity; No proof of property; No guilty knowledge; Consent; and so on. This being the case, the first step in arranging and pointing the evidence is to ascertain what can be disputed and what is incapable of denial. A prisoner cannot perhaps deny that he did a certain act. He is either justified then in law, or excused on the ground of insanity, or affirms that he had no guilty knowledge or intent, or that there was consent to what was done. It will be easily perceived, where the points of the prosecution will require to be made good. If you expend the force of your evidence to prove identity when the main defense is no guilty knowledge or intent to defraud, a rogue may escape from justice for want of mere forensic skill on your part, as he may from a policeman for want of handcuffs.

Do not think such an event unlikely to happen, or flatter yourself it will not happen to you; you will be a miracle of an advocate, or will never have a case at all, if it do not. The simple rule to observe then is, that you must take care, *while you are watching one hole, that the prisoner do not escape out of another.*

I once saw a man tried for embezzling money, the price of hay, which he had taken from a rick belonging to his employer and sold. There was no proof that he had ever had the money, and if he had, there was no proof that he had received it for or on account of his master. It was contended that if it was anything, it was stealing the hay. So he was acquitted and charged with stealing the hay. Argued that if it was anything it was embezzling the

money, for he had authority to sell the hay. Acquitted.
Not because he was not guilty.

§ 104. *Explaining Technicalities.*—As an example of the
necessity of a clear exposition of the charge against the
prisoner, and of lucid and well arranged statement of
facts in opening, together with a proper marshaling of evidence in proof, take the common case of a conspiracy, the
indictment for which runs to the following effect: That
Brown, Jones, Robinson and Tompkins, " being evil-dis-
posed persons, and wickedly devising and intending to defraud and prejudice certain persons hereafter mentioned, on
the 1st of April, did amongst themselves conspire, combine,
confederate and agree together, falsely and fraudulently to
cheat and defraud certain," etc.

Now, I doubt if one man in a hundred would ever know,
where unenlightened as to the legal meaning of legal phraseology, and only viewing the above words through the medium of common sense, when, if ever, he would be in a
position to say " guilty " or " not guilty."

§ 105. *Unnecessary Details.*—There is nothing more wearisome and useless than the dwelling on the extreme details
of a case, unless they are of importance. It may be that
some infinitesimally small matter may be of infinite importance; but a common-sense advocate will discern between
the important and the merely frivolous. I have seen hours
wasted in an examination before magistrates, where minutes
would have been sufficient for every purpose under the sun,
whether to ease the minds of your witnesses or to hang your
man — or somebody else's man — as the case might be.

Q. "Well, you went up to the door? " A. " Yes, sir" (meekly).

Q. "What did you do then — did any one else go with you? " A.
"Mrs. Brown, sir."

Q. "Mrs. Brown, who's Mrs. Brown? " A. "A neighbor, sir."

Q. "Where does she live? " A. " Next door to Mrs. Macdoodle's,
sir."

Q. "Well, how came Mrs. Brown to go? " A. "She came up with
me, sir."

Q. " Did you see where she came from? " A. "No, sir."

Q. "Well, you went to the door?" A. "Yes, sir."
Q. "Was anybody there?" A. "Yes, sir."
Q. "Who?" A. "A man."
Q. "Well, what did you do when you got to the door?" A. "I knocked, sir."
Q. "Did you knock more than once?" A. "No, sir."

Now, all this time has been taken up for no reason whatever, except to get that knock, and now we have it, it is perfectly useless, except to enable us to get inside where we want to get, for the purpose of examining the state of affairs there.

§ 106. *Cross-Examination.*— It is not necessary to repeat what has been said in a former part of this work with reference to the cross-examination for the prisoner. You may be sure that a copious shower of questions from your opponent will rain down some fact or other which will assist the prosecution. He must be a skilful advocate, indeed, who in a long cross-examination elicits no fact against himself, or lets in no evidence which will add a burden to his defense. You will, therefore, watch every question, and note the answer if it requires to be re-examined upon or commented upon in the summing-up or reply. I have seen men convicted by being defended by injudicious advocates, although they themselves may not have known it, and may have forced the questions which brought their destruction. The greatest lawyer that ever lived might be no advocate, and it is difficult to conceive of a very young advocate being a very good one. At the same time he must get experience somewhere; somebody must be the patient for him to practise upon for the benefit of the healthy body corporate. Still, he should learn as far as possible by the blunders of others rather than his own, and will have a fair opportunity of doing so, while engaged in a prosecution, by carefully watching and noting where a question is clumsy merely, and where it is wrong; by considering how questions should be asked, and, more important still, how they should be framed, so as to bring no harm to your case, and as much good as possible.

§ 107. *Reply.*— I should not think it necessary to say a word as to the reply in a criminal case, but that I have seen advocates so vehement, both in denunciation and " earnest · appeals," that one almost forgot that an unhappy wretch in custody was the occasion of it. Calm and temperate should at all times be the voice that asks for the condemnation of a fellow-creature. Every allowance should be made for the common infirmities that beset us : every portion of the case, not absolutely covered by the prosecution, should be left unmolested.

CHAPTER IX.—The Conduct of a Defense in a
Criminal Trial.

Although most of the remarks I have made apply equally
to criminal as to civil cases, it may be useful to give some
hints especially directed to the conduct of a criminal
defense.

§ 108. *Police Court Cases — When not to Defend.*— As
inexperienced advocates are frequently before the magistrates, in their professional capacity, it may not be without
some advantage if I make a few observations on the conduct of a case in those courts. The mode in which persons
charged with crime are defended at the Police Court has
often appeared to me a kind of preliminary retribution to
that which is to come. A young advocate, who has had
nothing of a more serious nature to defend than a charge of
drunkenness or assault, is suddenly called upon to *pose* before the public, in a case of wilful murder or some other
offense, where a committal is absolutely certain. How is he
to do justice to his client? There is only one way, and that
is, to hold his tongue. One would think advocacy the
easiest thing in the world, requiring neither training, knowl-

edge nor experience, to see how perfectly ready the young advocate is to step into the arena and do battle in the interests of the accused ; as if an advocate were made by being called to the bar, or admitted on the roll of solicitors, or by being articled as a solicitor's clerk. You might just as well expect the indentures of an apprentice to impart a knowledge of his handicraft. When a young solicitor or clerk is instructed to defend before the magistrate under the circumstances indicated, I should unhesitatingly advise him to preserve an unbroken silence. Otherwise he is almost sure to do mischief ; and the worst mischief is that he will most likely tie up the hands of the counsel engaged to defend before the ultimate tribunal.

It is possible that it may be desirable to have a fact or two upon the depositions ; but if so, it will require an advocate of some experience to ascertain what those facts shall be.   The greatest discretion should be used as to whether a question should be asked or not.   With a very few exceptions, no cross-examination should be administered when the case is to go for trial.

Instead of this course being pursued, a long cross-examination is often indulged in, or the young gentleman who thinks he is defending, puts as many questions as he can, under the impression that questioning is cross-examination, and then answers are elicited, detrimental, if not destructive, to every chance of acquittal.   For the purpose of convicting unfortunate wretches who are charged with offenses, the government need not establish public prosecutors while young advocates defend ; for these gentlemen can administer questions which the law forbids the prosecuting counsel to put ; and what is more, they can privately question the prisoner, and then by giving the information so obtained in the shape of questions to the witnesses, may display a knowledge of circumstances only consistent with the prisoner's guilt, as by showing that he was present at the scene of the crime, when probably the defense is to be an *alibi!*

I am afraid, too, that a good many innocent persons have

succumbed to a powerful cross-examination of this kind. Many juvenile advocates seem to consider that cross-examination consists in repeating the questions of the prosecution with the prefatory query—" Will you swear, sir,"— or by way of variation so as to show some degree of originality—" On your oath, sir? "

§ 109. *Same—When to Defend.*—There may, nevertheless, be cases where it is possible to avoid a committal by bringing all the facts before the magistrate. And this may be done sometimes even in the most serious charges. But no inexperienced advocate should be intrusted to defend under such circumstances. It was successfully done some time since in a case which attracted considerable attention from its remarkable circumstances. A woman had been murdered in a very shocking manner in a house of ill-fame in London. The police, as is customary, obtained the all-important clue, and it was, therefore, necessary to obtain a prisoner. They followed it up with that remarkable intelligence which always characterizes the " Force " in heavy cases ; and losing the clue for a moment on board a vessel which was outward bound, found it again almost immediately afterward in the spot where they had missed it. Instead, however, of arresting the man they were after, " from information received," they pounced upon an inoffensive and mild-looking clergyman, and charged him with wilful murder. Witnesses were soon obtained (the supply in London always being equal to the demand, whatever may be the commodity you require), who saw the Rev. gentleman leave the brothel where the deceased woman was found immediately after. The singular part of the story was, that he so exactly corresponded with the man whom they did *not see* leave the house, and whom the police were after in the first instance, and when they boarded the vessel. Of course, it was of the utmost importance that this gentleman should not be committed for trial, although a conviction would have been utterly impossible. It was consequently necessary to cross-examine the witnesses and to call evi-

dence. This was accordingly done, and it was clearly established that the reverend prisoner was perfectly innocent of
the charge ; that he was elsewhere at the time he was said
to have been in the street : and that there was no single circumstance even that required explanation.

Many cases there are where a judicious examination in
the first instance before the magistrate would insure the discharge of the accused, but in all these cases an advocate of
some experience should be retained. It may be taken as a
good rule, that where a case is going for trial, no defense
should be raised. It should be carefully watched, and a
question here and there judiciously interposed where something is certain to be obtained favorable to the accused.
Where the answer is doubtful, it should never be risked.
Severe cross-examinations and magnificent police-court
speeches can only be useful to the prosecution.

If, however, the case of the accused rests upon his calling witnesses, this will necessitate their being before the
magistrate, otherwise it will operate to the prejudice of the
defense at the trial. The prisoner, moreover, if they are
" bound over," will have the advantage of their expenses
being provided for, if the judge considers their evidence
material and trustworthy.

But if called, it is only necessary to give the outline of
their evidence, a full outline it may be, but the details
should be judiciously reserved. It is a good plan sometimes to have witnesses before the magistrate, and not call
them if you can avoid it. It takes the sting from the question, " Were you before the magistrate?" or " When were
you asked to give evidence?" This is very often, as
Brougham would say, " expedient."

§ 110. *What to do after Bill Found.*—Let it now be assumed that your client has been duly committed for trial,
and that a " true bill " has been found by the grand jury.
It is the first business of the counsel instructed to defend,
to see what charges the indictment contains. I am afraid
this duty is more often than not neglected by junior barris-

ters, and the consequence sometimes is that a prisoner is convicted on a bad indictment. It contains, perhaps, no offense known to the law, or it contains too many offenses; something is not set out which, should be, or there may be a great deal too much set out. There may in short be some "flaw," which, if taken advantage of in a proper manner, would insure the acquittal of the accused. This is by no means of such rare occurrence, notwithstanding the powers of amendment and the improved method of pleading, as to make it a matter of little moment to examine minutely the indictment.

Taking for granted that I am writing now to advocates who are good lawyers, I will assume that having carefully and critically perused the indictment, you know exactly what it contains, and I conclude that you will not move without strong necessity to have it quashed — (as this is by no means a safe proceeding)—that you will give no opportunity of amending, where, by taking objection at the proper time, you will compel your opponent to " elect " as to which of the counts he will proceed upon ; and that you will not prematurely take an objection, where you should reserve your attack for the forlorn hope of a motion in arrest of judgment.

§ 111. *Conduct of the Trial.*—These points having been carefully considered, and having thoroughly made up your mind as to what the defense is to be, remembering always that one good defense is better than two, you must now watch carefully the opening of the case for the prosecution. If your adversary open too much, it will be a point in your favor, " A guilty man," says Whately, " may often escape "—(I hope not often)—" by having too much laid to his charge ; so he may by having too much evidence against him, *i. e.*, some that is not itself satisfactory ; thus a prisoner may sometimes obtain an acquittal by showing that one of the witnesses against him is an infamous informer and spy, though perhaps, if that part of the evidence had been

omitted, the rest would have been sufficient for conviction."
—*Elements of Logic*, B. III, § 18.

Again, if your opponent inadvertently open a case, differing materially from the evidence of the witnesses or any
of them, it will be matter for observation which will not be
without its effect. It is not your business to object; you
do not know what he can prove, and if his proof fall short,
so much the better for your client. But you must narrowly
watch and object if counsel for the prosecution propose to
read any letter or document, or state any conversation
which, when the proper time comes, may not be admissible.
It is useless after the mischief has been done, and the impression made on the minds of the jury, for the judge to
say: "I shall tell the jury that that document or that conversation is not evidence, and that they are to dismiss it
from their minds." They *cannot* dismiss it from their
minds, and it is evidence, no matter whether you call it so
or not, when once before them, and will in all human probability have an influence on their judgment. It is like the
village lawyer telling the man that they could not put him
in the stocks; the irrefutable answer was: "But I am
here."

You must further take care that if you succeed in shut-
ting out a document. you exclude also all observations
upon it; for nothing is more unfair than to allude to a matter which is not in evidence, although it is often inadvertently done.

You will not trouble yourself to take down the evidence,
but as it is given, follow closely the deposition which the
witness has made before the magistrate—not with a view of
verbal criticism, or of establishing some trivial error or discrepancy; but to see that there are no material differences
or contradictions. These, if there be any, you will note and
call attention to in cross-examination. Unless you do this,
you will not be able to bring them to the mind of the jury.
But upon this subject I will say a word more particularly
hereafter, as the mode of doing it is a matter of the great-

est importance. With a wily witness the contradictions or variances may be artfully reconciled, or sufficiently so to impose upon the jury, unless great care is used in dealing with him. Your object is not to reconcile or give him an opportunity of explaining, but to impress the difference in the statements on the jury, and widen the gap rather than close it.

Besides remarking the difference between the testimony now given and that deposed before the magistrate, you must be equally careful to note the points of difference between the witnesses as well as the points of agreement. For observe : they must agree upon some point in your favor, and disagree as to something which is against you ; and indeed, any disagreement may be turned to advantage. With a little experience, and a good deal of observation, you will be able to distinguish between those matters of detail which sometimes betray perjured testimony, and details which are of no importance whatever ; as also to distinguish between mere inaccuracies in the evidence, arising from a slovenly habit of thought, and inaccuracies which are artfully contrived to deceive.

Inaccurate witnesses, when properly cross-examined, will often destroy the effect of the most accurate, as they will raise a doubt where none would otherwise exist. Inaccuracies, therefore, as to date, time, place, position of the parties, what was said, by whom, and other matters of a like kind, ought not to be overlooked, due regard being had to what was before observed as to mere discrepancies.

While you exercise the utmost vigilance to prevent the admission of matter which is not in evidence, care should be taken not to object to every question on that account, or because it may be put in a leading form or in a form that may be otherwise objectionable. Too many objections have the bad effect of wasting time and of raising an unjust suspicion in the mind of the jury.

That you should preserve the most even and calm demeanor in conducting a criminal defense, it is hardly necessary to observe. It is, indeed, a part, and no unimportant part, of your case. Irritation and querulousness are bad accompaniments of the best defense; and if you win, it will be in spite of them, and not by their assistance.

Let the worst be stated against you, but if possible, do not let the worst be proved. This must be your object in following closely the witnesses for the prosecution.

§ 112. *Rules for Cross-Examination.*—In cross-examination, I will repeat, the utmost care should be exercised; otherwise the facts, instead of being toned down, will stand out the more clearly. The danger is so great to the unfortunate object whose fate may be determined by an injudicious question, that you had better not cross-examine at all, if you have not perfect confidence in the line you are taking, and that the answers will not endanger his liberty or life. If you don't know what to ask, ask nothing.

I do not think any advocate, however clever he may be, should take upon himself a defense of any importance till he has had some experience. No man without it can cross-examine unless at great risk. He may ask questions and get answers, but he will be a wonderfully fortunate man if he do not inflict more damage upon his client than upon the witness. It has often occurred that after a spirited cross-examination by a young advocate, he has made the observation: "I think I have settled him, haven't I?" In the civility of my heart I have answered: "Yes, *I think you have.*" At the same time, I have no doubt we were speaking of two very different persons, he referring to the witness, and I thinking of his client. The best preparation a man can have to qualify himself to cross-examine is to study carefully the mode in which the best men proceed, and to acquire a knowledge of character, of human nature, of what is called "the world." One man may have a greater aptitude than another, but with the most gifted it requires years of training and observation to arrive at anything like perfection. With the ordinary individual, therefore, too much study cannot be given to acquiring sound knowledge of the art. While your cross-examination is proceeding, the counsel for the prosecution will watch for supplemental evidence, or for an opening through which he may drag some in. Frequently, he would have few materials to ask a verdict upon without this so-called cross-examination, and that being so, ask as little as you possibly can. If you cannot serve your client, avoid injuring him. Of course, the more ability you possess, and the more knowledge you acquire, the more you will be able to accomplish with the fewest questions.

At the commencement, it is a good plan to throw out one or two trifling and harmless questions, in order to ascertain the temper and feeling of the witness. It will tend also to put him on good terms with you, if there be a necessity for it. He may have been brought into court against his will and obliged to say what he has said; but with a little encouragement and a little gentle leading, he will probably follow you with the docility of a friendly witness. He may know a great deal more than he has said, and what he knows may throw much light on what has gone before. He may be a well-disposed witness after all, and likely enough will give a different color to the case. You know how greatly a coat of coloring changes the appearance of a bare wall, so it does the aspect of a bare fact. But if you commence by treating this witness in a hostile spirit, as though being a witness for the prosecution, he must necessarily be adverse in feeling to the prisoner, you may lose the benefit of all the kind things he may say in your behalf.

If on the other hand you perceive that a witness has a strong feeling in the matter, the less you have to do with him, the better. He will drive every nail home which the prosecution may not have struck forcibly enough. Ask him one question, he will answer as if you had asked him half-a-dozen, and every answer will be unfavorable. You might as well butt the witness-box with your head with a view to making evidence (and better for your client's sake), as question a witness of this kind. If you should get anything favorable, it will be by accident, and because he does not perceive the drift of your question. Everything you ask gives him the opportunity for a speech against the prisoner. If you can show his strong feeling by a well conceived question, it is all that you ought to attempt with a witness of this kind, unless, indeed, you can convict him of an untruth. These are your only chances with him.

But many hostile witnesses may be treated in a different manner according to their degrees of hostility and their temperament. You may sometimes destroy the effect of the evidence of an adverse witness by making him appear more hostile still. You may make him exaggerate or unsay something, and say it again. If you can not pull him off his high horse on one side, you may perhaps push him over on the other, and so long as you get him off, it does not much matter on which side you land him. Perhaps he will show himself spiteful, and lose his temper at the same time; if so, it will be in your favor, for juries dislike above all things to see spite in the witness-box. Every question must be asked with a view to *the theory of the defense.* Mere contradictions will not serve, unless you can show that they are in opposition to the probabilities of your case.

§ 113. *Cross-Examining the Police.* — I purposely reserved the consideration of the cross-examination of an important class of witnesses for this place, because it seemed to belong more particularly to this branch of advocacy. I refer to the police. Every one who conducts a defense in a criminal trial has to deal with police testimony, and as a class of evidence it figures more conspicuously in criminal courts than any other. Again, I shall commence by saying, as far as possible leave them alone. They are dangerous persons. They are professional witnesses, and in a sense that no other class of witnesses can be said to be. Their answers generally may be said to be stereotyped. All the ordinary questions may be answered scores of times by the well disciplined, " active and intelligent officer." He knows what you will ask him next, if you are no better than the rank and file of cross-examiners.

But try him with something just a little out of the common line by way of experiment. You see he looks at you, as though he had got the sun in his eyes. He can not quite see what you are about. And you must keep him with the sun in his eyes, if you desire to make anything of him.

To be effective with a policeman, your questions must be rapidly put. Although he has a trained mind for the witness-box, it is trained in a very narrow groove; it moves as he himself moves, slowly and ponderously along its particular beat; it travels slowly because of its discipline, and is by no means able to keep pace with yours, or ought not to be. You should not permit him to trace the connection between one question and another, when you desire that he should not do so. If you ask him whether it was a very dark night, and the darkness has nothing whatever to do with the issue, he will commence a process of reasoning as to your motive, and what might possibly be the effect of his answer. While this mental exertion is going on, interrupt him suddenly with a question you have a good reason for putting, and in all probability you will get something near the answer you require.

Policemen have a great deal of knowledge about the case, and a great deal of belief. The former you will find bad enough to deal with, but you must be careful not to elicit a large quantity of the latter; if you do, you may rest assured it will look so like a fact, that it will pass with the jury as such. You will be fortunate if it do not condense itself into a fact by the time you get it.

"What did you say when you apprehended the prisoner?" asked Jones, eager for the display of his severe ability in cross-examination. "Oh!" said the active and intelligent, "I forgot that, my lord"—(always taking my lord into his confidence). "I beg your lordship's pardon. I said, now Sykes, when you come out from doin' the last seven year, you told me you meant to turn over a new leaf, and 'ere you are agin." And there the counsel was again!

Unless you are certain of the answer, never under any
circumstances ask a policeman as to character. Your client
may have the best, but policemen have such a high standard
that no man in the dock can ever come up to it. The highest
character he can give a respectable man will be, that be
"does not know anything against him." I have often
heard them reprimanded for this answer by the judges, and
asked if they know anything in his favor. So if a man said
something while tipsy, and a policeman be asked : "He was
very drunk, wasn't he?" the answer will be : "He knowed
what he was about, sir."

Furthermore, it is dangerous to put "fishing" questions
to this class of witness. You are almost sure to catch the
wrong answer. Your safer course will be to cross-examine
for contradictions and improbabilities, and also where it is
necessary to give the witness the opportunity of denying
anything upon which you intend to contradict him. Cross-
examine for prejudices and as to opportunities, remembering always that there is often as much in the manner as in
the matter of cross-examination. and much more at times in
silence than in both. The policeman is not below human
nature generally. The parent of many of his faults is the
fact that police magistrates, as a rule, think he must be protected *by an implicit belief in his veracity.* As a natural
consequence, he falls into the error of believing in his own
infallibility.

§ 114. *When to Call Witnesses.*—Having completed your
duty in this respect, you will not be indiscreet enough to
"submit to the court there is no evidence to go to the jury"
if there be some ; but will consider whether you will call
witnesses, if you have not made up your mind at an earlier
stage of the case. If the evidence against you be weak,
and your own not strong, you ought not to call any. By
doing so, you will lose the last word, and what is perhaps of
far greater importance, run the risk of strengthening the
case against you on the cross-examination by the counsel for
the prosecution. This has often been done to the ruin of
the accused.

If at length you find that you ought to call witnesses, avoid calling too many : or rather, I should say, too many to the same subject-matter. One good witness is worth a dozen indifferent ones, and it is much more easy to get contradictions from a dozen than from two or three ; you always run the risk of witnesses contradicting one another, however truthful they may be. Remember, too, that a contradiction in your witnesses will be a much more serious affair than a contradiction among those of the other side ; for though the law presumes every man innocent until he be proved guilty, the jury presume every man on his trial to be guilty until the evidence fails to convince them. They will look in most cases with some suspicion upon the evidence for the defense, and every weak point in it will be magnified accordingly. In most cases, the witnesses for a prisoner either save or convict him. If they are good witnesses and honest, they are of inestimable importance ; but if they are shady, they will almost always be shaky, and infinitely worse than none at all.

§ 115. *The Speech for the Defense.*— But whether you call them or not, you will at last come to that very important part of your duty, namely, your speech on behalf of your client. How to speak it is not within the province of this work to teach, even if I were equal to the task. But I will assume that you have made that branch of advocacy your careful and assiduous study ; that you have attended debating societies, have spoken at public meetings, at the sea-side, and in your private room ; that you have practised the art with all the enthusiasm of one desirous of becoming eminent in your profession ; and with all the care that you could possibly bestow upon its cultivation ; that you have, in short, done all in your power to make yourself efficient in this fascinating branch of your professional duties.

You will now in the pleasantest manner, but with due gravity, commence your defense, and if the accused be a person of character, especially if he occupy any position in the social scale, you will do so by bringing these facts

prominently before the jury.   Nothing is more calculated to
engage their attention and enlist their sympathies than this,
besides which you excite as well as gratify their curiosity.
This feeling is akin to surprise, and nothing takes a firmer
hold of the attention.   At the same time you will almost
have excited the hopes of the jury on behalf of the accused.
The prosecutor will have passed from their minds, and a new
object presented itself, namely, that of a respectable, well-
educated man in the dock.   Imagination deepens the dis-
grace, and awakens still tenderer sympathies on his behalf.
They are sure to think, without any reminder on your part,
of those belonging to him, and of the hearts that beat in
unison with his own.   This is a part which should not be
hurried, for you want to give the feelings time to play.
Now bring forward the charge ; if it be one of enormous
guilt, or of a mean despicable kind, or one revolting to hu-
manity, what a contrast is produced between the character
and the crime !   There is an inherent improbability against
such a man committing such an offense !   That is a good
contrast to start with.

And, here again, be careful not to hurry the jury away
from so good a situation in the drama.   If you have performed this part of your defense with art and skill, you
have already prepared the mind for the impressions that are
to come.   A little lingering round the scene, without too
much to say, only to give time before you address yourself
to argument, will be beneficial.   Let them just have time
to contemplate the scene, and take in its misery.   Connected
with the improbabilities will be, possibly, absence of motive.
If so, the subject comes in naturally at this point.   If a
motive have been suggested, it must be grappled with, and
should be as soon as possible ; if not, it is a happy circumstance to be commented upon briefly, but with fervor.   The
jury, you will find, are following you sentence by sentence,
and word for word ; and the stronger your arguments, the
more intently they listen.   If now you point out how they
may acquit consistently with their oaths, they will feel in-

clined to do so. If you can explain away satisfactorily one or two awkward points in the evidence, the verdict will be yours. It has reduced itself to this already. Without the employment of any clap-trap you have gone a long way on your road. You have reached the feelings of the jury, and they wish to acquit.

Now it is your duty to show how it can be done. Bring up the evidence for the prosecution, not like a tender delicate creature, to be nurtured as it were by the counsel on the other side, but like a hideous thing to be looked at and put away out of sight. What is this evidence? Can you proceed to show that it is not consistent as a truthful story should be, but a patchwork performance of many pieces and many colors, a thing of no pattern? If so, it begins to lose its hold upon the jury; the improbabilities thicken and strengthen; there is increasing sympathy for the accused, as each juryman begins to think he may be the victim of a terrible mistake, or worse, of a horrible conspiracy! Encourage that feeling, not by saying that it is so, but by leading their minds to form the conclusion for themselves. Surely such a charge should, if made, be supported by conclusive and unimpeachable evidence, not such as is open to the observations you are making; not by evidence every part of which seems to be giving way under examination. And can you not point out how a man with an estimable character should not be destroyed by witnesses without any character at all? If there be one such among the witnesses for the prosecution, it will answer your purpose. It may be the prosecutor is a rapacious money-lender and the accused a man who borrows. The prosecutor may be a wrecker of homes, and the prisoner a man whose home is wrecked, and who is prosecuted for obtaining money by some false pretense upon a bill of sale. Accuser and accused may thus be brought into contrast. until at last the one will be looked upon with compassion and the other with contempt.

Perhaps you will discover some motive for the prosecuion apart from the divine "interests of justice;" if so, that is a kind of torpedo which, when you explode, will

blow the honest prosecutor out of the water. Having
reached this point, now will be the time for a display of
your powers of declamation. So you may prepare to use
them without delay, for you have Innocence in the dock and
Guilt in the witness-box! Such at least in the eyes of the
jury is the last situation of the drama. And here you may
resume your seat, while I drop the curtain.

§ 116. *Conclusion.* — If you have called witnesses, of
course, your obvious duty will be to point out the contrast
between their evidence and that of the witnesses for the
prosecution, as well as the fact of its being more compatible with the character of the accused. You will perceive
that character stands prominently forward again and again
without any ostentatious display. It should not be used
as though in so many words you asked the jury to acquit
because the prisoner bore a good character; it is of great
weight, where probabilities are balanced and circumstances
are doubtful—where they may receive a construction either
favorable or unfavorable to the person charged. It should
play its part like the principal character in a drama, appearing always at the right time and in the appropriate scene.
It is the one thing that has saved many a rogue from his
well-deserved doom, but it has also saved many an honest
man, unjustly charged, from ruin. It has preserved many a
family from misery and degradation. If you have this ally,
the enemy must be strong who defeats you. Of course,
there are cases where character does not come in; but there
are so many where it does, that it cannot be out of place to
insist upon it, as though there were hardly an exception.

I do not for a moment imply that facts go for little, where
the sympathies of a jury are strongly roused in a prisoner's
behalf. It is the view they are induced to take of the evidence through the medium of character, after balancing
the probabilities, that makes character of such inestimable
value. To rouse the feelings without laying hold of the
judgment would be idle. You might obtain a recommendation to mercy, but you would scarcely ever get a verdict of
acquittal.

CHAPTER X.—The Ethics of Advocacy.

"I hold every man a debtor to his profession," says Lord Bacon, "from the which as men of course do seek to receive countenance and profit, so ought they of duty to endeavor themselves, by way of amends, to be a help and ornament thereunto."

§ 117. *Old Prejudices.* — A popular opinion exists that the legal profession does not live up to this high standard of duty. The prejudice is of very respectable antiquity. For many generations the venal and unscrupulous advocate, and the knavish attorney, have been stock characters in that cheap satire, which, in default of originality, contents itself with iteration, and repeats to the sons the venerable jibes which have grown stale in the ears of their fathers. From the earliest English plays, down to Mark Meddle, in London Assurance, with his *"damages enormons,"* in broad farce and un-genteel comedy, there has been run through literature a succession of " limbs of the law," portrayed in colors not unworthy of " limbs of Satan," all as like to each other and with as little variation in their characteristics, as there is in the time-honored *facetiœ* of the circus clown.

A strong popular opinion is usually founded on a modicum of fact.   It is certainly true that in the " good old
times " in England, there prevailed among the lower grades
of legal practitioners a laxity of morals, which justified the
unfavorable views taken of the character of the profession.
Although it no longer deserves the obloquy cast upon it by
the misdeeds of these members long since dead and forgotten, still " the evil that men do lives after them," and the
sharp practice of mediæval attorneys yet stands to the discredit of their successors.

§ 118. *The Charges Stated.*— Unfavorable opinions of
the moral character of lawyers are not confined to the ignorant.   Many highly intelligent men have held, and some
still hold, that several practices usual at the Bar are contrary
to good conscience.   Pretermitting the stock charges of
cheating and extortion against attorneys in England, which
have no semblance of counterpart in American practice, the
allegations against lawyers are : First, that advocates offend
habitually against the higher law in undertaking causes
which they *know* to be unjust; second, that in their ad-
dresses to juries they make solemn personal asseverations
of the justice of their client's cause, and by skilful dissimu-
lation strive to persuade all men that they sincerely believe
statements which they do not believe.

§ 119. *Doctrine of the Casuists.*— The authorities for
the first of these charges are very respectable in point of
antiquity and otherwise.   Thomas Aquinas holds in general
terms that it is unlawful, morally, for a man to co-operate
with another in doing that which is wrong; and especially
that an advocate, who by his skill and experience enables a
suitor to obtain an unjust judgment, offends in like manner
and equal degree with the suitor himself.   Other casuists—
Ames, Morena, etc.—support the same view, and Feltham,
in his " Resolves," holds like language.   Later moralists
put the question on the simple ground that the advocate is
the agent of his client; that if the advantage gained is
against good conscience, the client could not rightly and

honestly obtain it for himself, and therefore his agent can not do so for him, because the stream can rise no higher -than the fountain. They deny the assertion of Erskine, and other eminent lawyers, that an advocate, being an officer of the court, cannot refuse his services to any one who will pay the usual fees for them. Their conclusion is that the lawyer's duty is in effect to try every case before he agrees to undertake it, and refuse it utterly, unless he is satisfied that his would-be client is certainly in good conscience, and probably in law, entitled to a judgment. Mr. David Hoffman, author of several valuable professional works, takes a similar view, going more into detail. He says that in a case which *in his opinion* he ought not to gain, he would never lend himself to an extorted compromise by which his client would get something, when in justice he should get nothing; that he would never take advantage of purely technical defenses, plead the statute of limitations based on the mere efflux of time, or set up the defense of infancy against an honest demand, if his client were able to pay.

§ 120. *The Other Side.*—On the other hand, many eminent writers hold a much less rigid view of professional duty. Erskine, in his defense of Tom Paine, takes a very decided position. He says: " If the advocate refuses to defend from what he thinks of the charge or the defense, he assumes the character of the judge; nay, he assumes it before the hour of judgment, and puts the heavy influence of perhaps a mistaken opinion into the scale against the accused, in whose favor the benevolent principles of the English law make all presumptions, and even compel the judge himself to be his counsel.'' This was a case of criminal law, but upon the leading principles of the rigid moralists heretofore cited, it must abide a like decision with civil cases. That principle is, that the advocate is himself the judge of the justice of the cause offered. If it be righteous, he must take it. If not, he must refuse, and there is no reason why it should be more venial for him to aid a malefactor to escape punishment which he has deserved, than to secure money to

a client to which he is not entitled. Most people, however,
take a much more reasonable view, and make a distinction
between cases in which a man is fighting for his life or lib-.
erty, and those which involve only a sum of money. In
most of our States, the law in its tenderness for persons accused of crime, *compels* counsel to render their services to
such defendants as may be too poor to pay the customary
fees.

§ 121. *Bad [Causes.* — On the subject of what are
called "bad causes," Dr. Johnson's authority is sometimes
cited, but his opinion is (for him) singularly weak and in-
conclusive. He was asked by Boswell: "What do you
think of supporting a cause which you know to be bad?"
"Sir," replied the sage, "you do not know it to be bad
till the judge determines it.   *   *   *   You are to state
the facts fairly; but an argument which does not convince
you, may convince the judge;   *   *   *   then you are wrong,
and he is right." This is, under deep submission, very
nearly nonsense. If the cause is "bad" in morals, the solution slips, like an ill-dealt card, underneath the table, for
the judge does not decide causes in that sense at all. He
decides *law*, not morals. If the cause is "bad" in law,
Dr. Johnson's rule of practice is distinctly immoral, and is so
held by every practitioner above the grade of pettifogger or
shyster. When a lawyer thinks his client's case is bad in
law, his duty is very clear, fully understood, and daily
acted on in the profession. Simply tell him that you think
the law is against him. If he accepts your opinion, that
ends the matter. If he persists, and craves the luxury of
a lawsuit, indulge him by all means, and you can pocket
your fee with a clear conscience.

As to the duty of an advocate with reference to causes
morally "bad," it may be premised that in civil practice there is no duty incumbent upon him to appear in
any case which he may choose to decline. He must appear, it is true, for the poor in criminal cases, if assigned
to that duty by the court. Beyond this, there is no

law, moral or civil, that restricts his free agency. He is not a common carrier, bound to fetch and carry for every comer, • nor yet a scapegoat to bear into the wilderness the sins and follies of indefinite and miscellaneous clients. If, therefore, he appears as the champion of fraud, iniquity, or oppression, he can plead no professional duress. He is no more bound to do a mean or wicked thing than any body else, and is as much amenable to the moral law as unprofessional people. So far, therefore, as concerns " bad causes," he is to be judged by the same standard as other persons acting as agents or under delegated authority. The practical difficulty in this matter is, that it is often almost impossible to say what is the real character of a cause, until it has nearly run its course. Lawsuits, in this respect, have no earmarks. Under the English system, the barrister derives all his information as to the facts from the brief prepared by the attorney. Here he confers directly with the client, who is very seldom frank, and rarely discloses moral obliquities. A client is sometimes as hard to get the truth out of, as the most recalcitrant witness ; there is always an *arriere pensee* of unfavorable facts held back, because of the silly hope that if he says nothing about them, even to his own counsel, nobody else will. This ostrich policy is not over-wise, but clients are not *necessarily* wise — indeed, some people think the fact that they are clients at all is a strong presumption against their wisdom. In a very large proportion of cases, therefore, the moral character, so to speak, of a lawsuit is not developed until after it has made considerable progress ; certainly not until after counsel has been retained on both sides.

§ 122. *Justice and Law.*— Natural justice and positive law are so intermingled, that it often becomes difficult to decide which controls the point in question. This case may be cited : A. made his will, disinheriting his heir, a collateral relation. The will is found to be, by a pure technicality, defective in execution and invalid. It is held by some moralists that as A. owned the property, had a right to do as he

pleased with his own, intended the devisee to have it, tried
to give it to him, and failed only by a mistake, it was immoral and wrong for the heir, being only a collateral relation, and having no claim upon the bounty of the deceased,
to take advantage of the imperfection of the will, and claim
the estate by descent.   Now, this is a case into which neither morality nor natural justice enter in the slightest
degree.   It is a matter of pure, absolute, positive law. A.'s
right to make a will at all is the creation of positive law,
which annexed to the exercise of the right certain conditions,
one of which he failed to observe.   The same positive
law empowers the heir to take the estate by descent, if A.
shall fail to make a valid will, and his right to inherit is of
as high a dignity as A.'s right to devise.   There is not a
scintilla of moral right or justice in this case on either side:
The heir had no claim upon A. for the property at his death ;
A. had no correlative right to demand of the heir obedience,
or duty, or regard for his wishes.

§ 123. *Hard Cases.*— It will be found that many of the
so-called bad causes are of this character, and a large ma-
jority of them are of a class which might be described as
cases hard — *but fair*.

A case of hardship that does not fall within one or the
other of these categories may be mentioned : A man in a
Southern State executed his will some years before the civil
war.   He devised his land to his sons, and bequeathed his
slaves to his daughters.   The will evidently contemplated
equality among his children, for their respective shares of
his estate were about equal in value at the date of the will.
During his lifetime the slaves were emancipated, but from
procrastination and imbecility, the will remained unaltered,
and upon his death his sons received his whole estate, and
his daughters received — nothing.

§ 124. *Fraudulent Devices.*— Of course, there is an infinite variety of fraudulent devices, which very properly come
under the designation of " bad causes," but it is not incumbent upon you to presume against your client's fair dealing ;

on the contrary, he, in common with all men, is entitled to
the proverbial presumption of innocence. It is not your
duty to try his case in the court of conscience before you
try it in a court of law, or laboriously to investigate all the
circumstances, with the view of discovering any evidence of
foul play that may be lurking in any of its convolutions.
If his case is fair upon its face, and you should have no
good reason *aliunde* for suspecting his good faith, you are
justified in accepting his cause. The true guides in such
questions are common sense and honor. The first will prevent you from going into Quixotic extremes, and doing
works of supererogation in the way of conscientious self-
denial ; the other will keep you clear of participation, personal or professional, in the dishonorable practices of a.
knavish client.

§ 125. *About False Asseverations.*—The second charge
which has been made against the profession is, that lawyers.
in their addresses to juries often make false assertions of
the justice of their client's cause, or their individual belief
in its justice, and in this offend against morality and good
conscience. Is there anything, it is asked, in the relation
of client and counsel which releases the latter from the
obligation, incumbent upon him as upon all men, to tell the
truth? Why has he a right, by vehement asseverations of
the truth of statements which he does not believe, to throw
the weight of his personal character into his client's scale,
and seek to influence the jury in his favor? These false
asseverations, it is argued, have been believed, or they have
not. If they have, and have influenced the jury, the client
has gained an advantage by what amounts in effect to false
testimony, the counsel being the false witness. If it has
not been believed, the advocate has tried to influence the
jury improperly and failed, and is as guilty in point of intention as if he had succeeded. At best he has, following
a bad fashion, and without the intention of deceiving, put
on the habiliments of falsehood, and posed in a court of
justice, not, it is true, as a false witness, but as the " coun-

terfeit presentment " of one, thus lowering the dignity of
the profession.

§ 126. *Brougham and Dr. Paley.*—The most extreme
advocate of the privileges of counsel was Lord Brougham,
who, in his speech in Queen Caroline's case, defined the duties of an advocate thus : " An advocate — by the sacred
duty of his connection with his client—knows in the discharge
of that office but one person in the world — that client —and
none other. To serve that client by all expedient means ;
to protect that client at all hazards and costs to all others
(even the party already injured) and amongst others to
himself, is the highest and most unquestioned of his
duties." If this is a correct exposition of the privileges
of an advocate, it is conclusive upon the question, for " all
expedient means " would include much more than the objectionable practice under consideration. Lord Brougham's
authority, however, on this point is very generally con-
troverted. He was speaking under very exciting and
extraordinary circumstances ; defending the character of a
woman against the inveterate enmity of a great King, he
would naturally arrogate to himself the broadest privileges
possible. Where the character of a woman or the life of a
man is at stake, an advocate would naturally seek to avail
himself of all the means which God and nature had put into
his hands. Cooler critics, however, refuse to recognize the
validity of this charter, " wide as the winds," which Lord
Brougham had conferred upon the profession, and restrict
the privileges of counsel within much narrower limits.

The most usual defense of this obnoxious practice is that
these false asseverations are privileged, being a mere fashion
of speech, sanctioned by long custom, and innocent, because
nobody expects the truth from a lawyer " on his legs " in a
court of justice. Dr. Paley is the standing authority for this
doctrine. He says : " There are falsehoods that are no
lies, *i. e.*, not criminal " (among others) " a criminal
pleading not guilty ; an advocate asserting the justice, or
his belief in the justice of his client's cause ; *   *   *   *

no confidence is destroyed, because none is reposed; no promise to speak the truth is violated, because none is given." To say nothing of the unsavory company in which the defense places the advocate—ill-starred conjunction of the bar and the dock!—it is not very flattering to the profession to be thus acquitted of lying, because nobody will believe them.

§ 127. *The Courvoisier Case.*—A very thorough discussion of this subject took place in England about forty years ago. In May, 1840, Lord William Russell, an old man, was found murdered in his bed, evidently assassinated for his money and other valuables. His valet, Courvoisier, was suspected and tried. He was defended by Mr. Philips, an eminent barrister, who, as he asserts, fully believed that his client was innocent, because the evidence against him was purely circumstantial, and there was strong reason to suspect that certain policemen, actuated by greed for the large rewards that had been offered, had conspired to effect the conviction of the prisoner, in order, as Mr. Philips strongly expressed it, "to divide the reward money upon Courvoisier's coffin."

In the course of the trial, which lasted three days, Courvoisier suddenly demanded an interview with his counsel, confessed that he had murdered his master, but insisted that they should defend him to the uttermost. This Mr. Philips proceeded to do, and his manner of discharging his duty as an advocate subjected him to very grave charges. Courvoisier was found guilty and duly executed, and after his confession to his counsel had been made public, Mr. Philips was charged by the Examiner newspaper, and afterward by other publications, with having, after Courvoisier's confession, asseverated his belief in that person's innocence, calling God to witness his sincerity, in the most impassioned manner. The further charge that, knowing Courvoisier to be the sole murderer, he imputed guilt to the female servants, was denied and not sustained by proof. On *this* point there can be no question. Had he been guilty of that outrage, no punishment could have been too severe.

There was of course a defense against the allegation, that he had professed belief in Courvoisier's innocence; the controversy, conducted with the utmost acrimony, ran for months through the leading newspapers and other periodicals of England, and was revived ten years afterward by the Examiner in a series of articles assailing Mr. Philips. On this point there was a question of fact. The reports of the trial differed materially from each other, and it was by no means certain what Mr. Philips *did* say on the trial. He always denied that he had professed any belief in the prisoner's innocence. Of course, public opinion remained unsettled, but with a preponderance in favor of Mr. Philips' innocence of any impropriety or unprofessional conduct.

§ 128. *Its Moral.* — Now, the "moral" of the Courvoisier case is this: It is not, or at least should not be, professional for an advocate to obtrude upon a jury in any case, civil or criminal, his personal knowledge or belief. If he states what purports to be a fact as of his knowledge, he is testifying without having been sworn. If he states his belief only, he is giving his client the benefit of his individual reputation for sincerity and acumen. This is neither his duty nor his client's right. It is unjust that an advocate shall say in effect to a jury, "I am a man of great ability, deep learning, extensive experience, and *I* believe this; *you* should do so too." It is unfair if he does believe it, and nefarious if he does not. It is idle to say that such statements should not influence a jury. They should not, but they sometimes *do;* and so far as they do, they are in derogation of the duty of the jury to find "according to the evidence."

§ 129. *Judicial Rebuke.* — This practice is sometimes justly reprobated by courts. An acute, but severe, judge once said to a jury: "The counsel has said 'I think this,' and 'I believe that.' A counsel has no right to say what he thinks or what he believes; but since he has told you, gentlemen, his belief, I will tell you mine—that if you were to believe him, and acquit his client, he would be the very first man in this court to laugh at you.''

§ 130. *The Sum of the Matter.*— The sum of the whole matter is, that there is no code of morality applicable especially to any profession or avocation. The tradesman can not plead the custom of the trade as an excuse for misrepresentation of the quality of goods; the mechanic, for slipshod and "slighted" work; the draper, for imitation articles sold as genuine; the grocer, for "watering the brandy, and sanding the sugar, before he goes to prayers," as the old joke has it; the apothecary, for dispensing adulterated drugs; and the advocate has no better right than these, for claiming exemption from moral responsibility for his acts in the course of his business. He can not lay the blame on his client; the principle of *respondeat superior* is not recognized in the court of conscience. It is the *man*, and not the advocate, whose responsibility is in question. One of the warlike baron-bishops of the middle ages was taxed by the all-licensed jester of his household with certain offenses against moral law. In reply he claimed the benefit of clergy. He was a bishop, as well as a knight, he said, and the devil had no power over him. "But," retorted the fool, "when the devil flies away with the knight, what will become of the bishop?"

CHAPTER XI —AMERICAN FORENSIC ORATORY.

§ 131. *Few American State Trials.*— It has not been the fortune of the American bar to contribute by its forensic ability to the establishment of civil or political liberty. In England, the legal profession has often been arrayed against arbitrary power, and proved itself a fearless and formidable champion of popular rights — notably in the trial of the bishops in the dark days of James II., and the question of "General Warrants," and the prosecutions founded on the law of libel in the closing years of the last century. Here the government has rarely come into conflict with the liberty of the citizen, and still less has it sought to make the judiciary an instrument of oppression. Lacking the lofty themes which inspired Somers, Erskine, and others, American advocates have nevertheless proved themselves not unworthy rivals of those great masters of forensic oratory.

§ 132. *But other Exciting Themes.*— In this day, with our security for life and property, our modern organization of society, the more certain enforcement of laws, and more methodical arrangement of all the affairs of life, there arise few occasions when the higher flights of forensic eloquence become appropriate. One can not argue, in the '*Quousque tandem Catilina*' style a case involving contribu-

malice. Let him draw rather a decorous, smooth-faced, bloodless de-
mon, a picture in *repose* rather than in *action*; not so much an example
of human nature in its depravity and in its paroxysms of *crime*, as an
infernal nature, a fiend in the ordinary display and development of his
character."

In the argument which follows he is thoroughly master
of the situation ; makes no allegation which he does not sub-
stantiate, either by the declaration of a witness or a fair de-
duction from the facts of the case established by the testimony, leaves no point available for effective reply, and ex-
cludes the possible accuracy of any hypothesis inconsistent
with the guilt of the prisoner.   As a chain of ratiocination,
it is absolutely impregnable.

Webster was a man of remarkable congruities.   His
manner was a perfect exponent of personal dignity.   His
massive head, his imposing figure, his few, slow, impressive
gestures accorded well with his forceful nature.   His voice
was full, flexible and skilfully modulated.   There is something very majestic in this perfect fitness for a special sphere.
This matter of personal endowment is of infinite importance
to the orator, more than to any other suitor for public favor.
The author is like the enchanted knight of old, who strode
invisible through hostile camps — the world sees only the
result of his work.   The actor has, to sustain him, stage
accessories, costume, music, the talent of the play-wright.
The orator stands alone, the audience before him and the
word in his heart.

§ 135. *Choate.* — Mr. Webster possessed even the rare
discernment to understand the limitations of his own
powers as an orator.   It is said that he was specially
sparing of ornamentation and peculiarly disposed to apply
the test of reason, cold and neutral, whenever he was opposed to Rufus Choate.   He would not vie with the splendid
diction of his gifted compeer.   He was wont to ridicule to
juries these flights of fancy, and to strip from the question
the graces of Choate's rhetoric, which could idealize a mere
mop-stick of a fact into a gay and gallant Chevalier Feath-
ertop.   This, however, was the result of his solicitude, lest

(11)

the jury be unduly beguiled. In his own proper person
he entertained a generous admiration of Choate's resistless
eloquence, which swayed the hearts of men, as the " breeze
bends the barley."

" This," Mr. Webster once declared to a colleague, " is
reason, impelled by passion, sustained by legal learning,
and adorned by fancy."

When these distinguished advocates chanced to be oppo-
nents, a greater contrast cannot well be imagined.   Choate
was alert in every fibre.   He was like a personified passion,
and every gesture was expressive of his exalted excitement.
He would shake his long, quivering nervous fingers above
his head.   He would advance toward the jury with an intent eye and an impressively lowered voice.   Sometimes he
would draw his figure to its full height, and fling his right
arm aloft with so exultant a motion, that it gave an effect as
if he had suddenly sprung into the air.   Prejudice, law,
right, reason went down before that whirlwind of words.
There are instances of logic sufficiently stout and tough,
and facts so deeply rooted as to withstand it—but they were
rare.

When a speaker is in the midst of an impassioned address, let but some allusion, charged with an unconsciously
ludicrous suggestion, escape him— and down he comes with
the velocity of a collapsed balloon.   The boundaries between the pathetic and the absurd are ill-defined, and to
enact successfully the " pity my sorrows " *röle*, one must
needs
> " ——distinguish and divide
> A hair 'twixt south and southwest side."

No one so well understood the lachrymose possibilities of
a jury as Rufus Choate.   He is reputed to have availed
himself of this knowledge.

" Why, that man can *cant* his countenance so as to draw
tears from your eyes," declared an indignant suitor whose
interests had suffered from the advocate's eloquence.

The solidity of Choate's genius, his deep and thorough

knowledge of the law, his quickness of perception, his skill
in the examination of witnesses and marshalling of facts,
his immense capacity for professional toil dwarf in the estimation of the bar the grace of his rhetoric. But to the
general public the style of expression and illustration that
embellishes his cogent argument is so brilliant, that the
fioriture, to use a musical term, quite overpowers the ster-
ling merit of the theme — and it certainly renders his few
printed efforts, although on subjects as dead as Ariovistus,
interesting essays—

> ———*miscuit utile dulci*
> *Lectorem delectando pariterque monendo.*

His prancing " substantive and six," which he was wont
to drive so recklessly through all his harangues, was conspicuously absent from his social witticisms, of which Mr.
E. P. Whipple in his recent admirable biographical essay
has preserved specimens that rival the brilliance of Sheridan. Choate's sarcasm has the sharp-shooter's accuracy,
and it has, too, a wonderful spontaneity. It is even more
remarkable in lacking that usual concomitant of satire, a
covert malignity.

§ 136. *S. S. Prentiss.* — The adroit and unerring tact
which was so marked a factor in Choate's forensic success,
was also possessed by S. S. Prentiss. He was endowed in a
notable degree with that fine inexplicable sixth sense, which
adopts instinctively the right phrase, the gesture, even the
very glance, certain to convince the reason, fascinate the
imagination and enthrall the heart, which is a pre-requisite
of oratory. In the delicate matter of seeking to conciliate
a jury — a difficult task and liable to be grossly patent —
Prentiss pre-eminently displayed this tact.

"My clients have come before you for justice. They have fled to
you, even as to the horns of the altar, for protection," he said, when he
stood up to address the jury in the Wilkinson case. "Here, in the heart
of Kentucky, they have sought and obtained an unprejudiced and impartial jury. You hold in your hands the balance of justice; and I ask
and expect that you will not permit the prosecution to cast extraneous
and improper weights into the scale against the lives of the defendants.

You constitute the mirror whose office it is to reflect in your verdict the law and the evidence which have been submitted to you. Let no foul breath dim its pure surface and cause it to render back a broken and distorted image. Let not the learned counsel who conducts the private part of this prosecution act the necromancer with you, as he did with the populace in the City of Louisville, when he raised a tempest which his own wizard hand could not have controlled. Well might he exclaim in reference to that act like the foul spirit in Manfred:—

> ' I am the rider of the wind,
> The stirrer of the storm;
> The hurricane I left behind,
> Is still with lightning warm.'

Aye, so it is with lightning warm;' but you, gentlemen, will perform the humane office of a conductor, and convey this electric fluid safely to the earth."

His speech in this same case furnishes specimens of the most bitter invective ever heard in a court of justice. It is said to be, however, as it is printed, the merest ghost of itself. Prentiss was emphatically an orator, and, shorn of the charm of his delivery, the mere words are in comparison lifeless. He himself said that he would rather make ten speeches than write one. The play of expression, the inflections of his finely modulated voice, the glance of his eye were such potent adjuncts to his efforts that he has been admonished by a crowd: "Look this way, Prentiss!" " Turn round here!" etc.

His fame as an orator and an advocate, like that of Rufus Choate, in popular esteem overshadowed his character as jurist. But despite his political absorptions and his bustling life, his legal attainments were great, and won full recognition from the bar and bench. Indeed, Judge Sharkey, who was for many years Chief Justice of Mississippi, and had therefore the best opportunities for sounding Prentiss' depth, once declared to the editor of this work that he considered S. S. Prentiss, notwithstanding his youth, a " profound lawyer."

§ 137. *Henry.*— Patrick Henry, however, hid no light of legal learning under a bushel. Without reading and without logic, his sphere was necessarily circumscribed. He was the orator, and the orator only. His influence died with his matchless voice and impassioned action, and he left nothing behind him save a few patriotic sentences, which, however, will live as long as the language in which they were uttered. Mr. Jefferson says of him: "He spoke as Homer wrote. * * * I never heard anything that deserved to be called by the same name with what flowed from him." Juries responded to his control as the trained steed obeys the rein. "Patrick Henry couldn't save him," was for a long time an expression in common use to denote the desperate straits of a criminal.

Dr. Archibald Alexander, who heard some of his greatest speeches, thus analyzes Henry's oratory:

"The power of Henry's eloquence was due, first, to the greatness of his emotion and passion, accompanied with a versatility which enabled him to assume at once any emotion or passion which was suited to his ends. Not less indispensable, secondly, was a matchless perfection of the organs of expression, including the entire apparatus of voice, intonation, pause, gestures, attitude, and indescribable play of countenance. In no instance did he ever indulge in an expression that was not instantly recognized as nature itself; yet some of his penetrating and subduing tones were absolutely peculiar, and as inimitable as they were indescribable. These were felt by every hearer in all their force. His mightiest feelings were sometimes indicated and communicated by a long pause, aided by an eloquent aspect and some significant use of the finger."

§ 138. *Wirt.*— Indissolubly connected with the name of Henry is that of his biographer, Wirt, who displayed great eloquence and learning at the bar, notably in the prosecution of Aaron Burr.

§ 139. *Clay.*—In this trial was also engaged Henry Clay, a man of wonderful magnetism and universal genius, equally great on the stump, before a jury, and in the gravest councils of the nation. He himself, however, was disposed to account for his pre-eminence as an advocate and an orator on more prosaic grounds than natural endowment.

"I owe my success in life," he said once in addressing a graduating class of law students, "to one single fact, namely, that at an early age I commenced and continued for some years the practice of daily reading and speaking the contents of some historical or scientific book. These off-hand efforts were sometimes made in a cornfield; at others in the forest, and not unfrequently in some distant barn, with the horse and ox for my only auditors.   It is to this early practice of the art of all arts, that I am indebted for the primary and leading impulses that stimulated my progress, and have shaped and moulded my destiny."

Thus he placed before himself at the outset of life a worthy ambition, and pursued it with zeal.   So strong a fascination did the career he had chosen exert upon him, and so devoutly did his every thought turn toward it, that in his first effort outside of a barnyard, he inadvertently addressed a youthful debating society as " Gentlemen of the jury," to the great delight of that sage body.   But as Henry Clay assumed more and more the character of states-man, the bar gradually lost him, and the greatest efforts of his life do not properly appertain to forensic oratory ; so with a host of others — Calhoun, Crittenden, Benton, Hayne, Bell, Grundy,

"What! will the line stretch out to the crack of doom?"

§ 140. *American Love of Oratory.*— Americans are a peculiarly speech-loving and speech-making people.   Men who can speak, and the multitude who merely think they can, avail themselves of every decent pretext, from the inauguration of a president to the presentation of a cane, for an address, an oration, or more modestly but not less lengthily, " a few remarks."   The speaker usually ad-dresses a docile and willing audience ; for widely diffused as is the *cacoethes loquendi* in the orators of the day, commen-surate with it is the *cacoethes audiendi* on the part of their hearers.

To a degree, culture and *exigeant* taste are arrayed against the orator.   If it be under a certain grade of excellence, the oration is regarded simply as a work of art, and is criticised as such, as coolly as if it were a statue or a painting. Above that grade, however, nature resumes its sway, and the heart of the critic becomes as fully amenable to its in-fluence, as is the heart of the clown to the " spread eagle " style of elocution which appeals to his coarser instincts.

CHAPTER XII.—This Honorable Court.

§ 141. *Classes of Judges.* — The relations between the bar and the bench have a very important influence, as well upon the due administration of justice, as upon the professional fortunes of .the individual advocate. As judges in this country are usually selected by the *chance-medley* of popular elections, it often happens that men, who by nature and training are unfitted for them, obtain judicial offices. It is profitable, therefore, for the advocate to study carefully, and understand thoroughly, the idiosyncracies of the judge before whom he habitually appears. The ideal judge is, of course, an impersonation of the law, calm, patient, inflexible and *infallible.* The actual judge is subject to a few — a very few — human weaknesses. He is sometimes captious, impatient and irritable, and often entertains unreasonable and extreme views on particular subjects. Some are unduly rapid in the trial of causes, the testimony is huddled in, too little time allowed for argument, and cases disposed of without proper consideration ; others err in the opposite direction, are dilatory in all things, permit interminable argument on minor questions, and consequently the docket gets sadly in arrears ; cases, for want of time, go over from term to term, and justice, though not denied, is delayed.

Judges are frequently imbued with overweening partiality for particular principles. Sometimes one is what may be

called a " woman's judge," because it is with the utmost
difficulty that he can be induced to make a ruling adverse to
the interests of a *feme covert*. Sometimes he is a " cred-
itor's judge," because of his exceeding strictness in marking
what may have been done amiss by debtors—in the way of
fraudulent conveyances and the like. This failing, however,
" leans to virtue's side ;" but there are judges so extreme,
that in Portia's place, they would have awarded to Shylock
his pound of flesh upon the ground that a deed must be
construed most strongly against the grantor, and that the
concession of the flesh carried with it by implication the
blood necessary to make the grant effectual. There is, or
rather was, also the " debtor's judge." Under the influence of intense and wide-spread financial pressure, legisla-
tures, in former times, chartered relief banks and passed
stay laws, and judges granted injunctions profusely, and
favored defenses of more than doubtful legality. These
times have passed, and that style of judge is extinct — for
the present.

§ 142. *Corrupt Judges.* — Of corrupt judges, nothing
whatever need be said. There was once a book written de-
scriptive of Iceland ; the heading of Chapter XIV was
" Concerning the Snakes of Iceland ; " the body of this
(the shortest chapter on record) was as follows : " There
are no snakes in Iceland." To the credit of the profession
it may be affirmed as positively, that there are no corrupt
judges in the United States. Gloves stuffed with gold
pieces do not now, as in Lord Bacon's day, come to the
hands of judges. They touch no money but their salaries,
often inadequate compensation for their services.

§ 143. *Respect for the Judicial Office.*—It seems a mere
platitude to say that an advocate should never fail in respect
for the judicial office, and for the person filling it ; yet, in
view of the frequent fines imposed for contempt of court,
that sort of admonition is not wholly superfluous. It often
happens that, when a judge is impatient and irritable, and the
advocate over-zealous and excited, a ruling of supernatural

stupidity, as the latter considers it, will overthrow his equilibrium and precipitate a collision. In that sort of contest he is always at a disadvantage; his judicial opponent holds the winning hand, and if he does not proceed to the length of actual punishment for contempt, will probably otherwise make his displeasure felt. It is a grave misfortune for an advocate to be on bad terms personally with the presiding judge, and such relations should be sedulously avoided by all means consistent with self-respect. Consciously or unconsciously, generally the latter, the judge will incline to rule adversely to the obnoxious counsel, and in effect throw upon him the *onus*, so to speak, of establishing his propositions to a certainty, not required of other lawyers. Hence, under all circumstances, and especially in his relations with the bench, the advocate should hold his temper under the strictest control. A perfect command of himself in this respect is a quality as indispensable to a lawyer, as strong nerves and a steady hand to the operating surgeon. There have been good lawyers, even great lawyers, who were irritable and excitable,— they have been good and great lawyers in spite of this capital defect. An advocate in court, and especially with reference to the bench, should strictly preserve his official character of an officer of the court, indulging as little as may be in any remarks touching his individual personality. He should endeavor to keep his business so well in hand that he has rarely occasion to ask a favor from the indulgence of the bench or the courtesy of the bar; for a man never appears to so little advantage, as in asking a relaxation of rules to avert the consequences of his own negligence. In this connection, it may as well be said that an advocate should spare no pains to be always ready for trial when his case is called. In many courts it is the habit of the bar to waste much time, after a case has been called, before it is " taken up." There is a consultation between client and counsel on one side or both, witnesses are out of place and have to be called or sent for; lawyers are not in court; the " papers " are in

the lawyer's desk, and have to be brought to the court-
house.   Under these circumstances judicial patience waxeth
very thin, and there is a peremptory order to " try, or continue."   Now he, who by dilatory habits frequently thus
impedes the course of justice, becomes the reverse of a fa-
vorite with the judge, and will probably suffer in the judicial appreciation of his professional efforts.   The court will
not *mean* to do him an injustice, but will nevertheless be
influenced by his habitual neglect of his business.   Theoret-
ically, the court decides by the weight of argument, without
reference to the speaker who propounds it ; practically, the
personality of the advocate more or less sways the judicial
mind. .

§ 144. *Patience and Impatience.*— In a jury trial before
an impatient judge it is necessary for counsel to be
especially on their guard.   In this country, and particularly
in the rural districts, witnesses are not examined rapidly.
After each question there is sometimes a consultation between counsel and client, and when an advocate avails himself too freely of the large liberty he enjoys in this respect,
he is sharply called to order by the court, and sometimes
loses a point he might have made.   It is not, however, so
much in the examination of witnesses, as in the argument of
legal questions, that the impatience of judges is improperly
manifested.   Some judges interrupt continually, propound-
ing questions and stating arguments adverse to the views of
the speaker, until the speech of the advocate becomes a
mere wrangle between judge and lawyer.   This is unfair ;
for to say nothing of disconcerting the young and inexperienced, it disarranges the order of the speaker's ideas,
compelling him, out of due season, to answer the judicial
interpellation, whereas later, and in another connection, he
could much more effectually have done justice to the subject.   When this sort of scene takes place, as it sometimes
does, in the presence of the jury, as in the argument of a
point of evidence, or other collateral issue, it is particularly
objectionable.   It conveys to the mind of the jury the idea

that the court is snubbing the counsel, and seriously damages him and his cause in their estimation. Now, "no offense to the General, or any man of quality," this is an evil that should be reformed altogether. There are only two cases in which the court should ever interrupt the speech of an advocate; one, when he is arguing a point on which the court has made up its mind in his favor,—to save time it is well to stop him, and request him to turn his attention to some other part of the case; the other, when the court does not understand his position, and an explanation is desired. Beyond this, there should be no interruption; and even within these limits, the fewer, the better.

When an adverse ruling is made, especially if it be wholly unexpected, the losing lawyer sometimes permits himself to be placed in an undignified position. In asking an explanation he renews the argument, getting up a discussion with the judge, and proceeding to such length that, besides losing his point, he loses his temper. This is a pitiable blunder; for a man is never so absurd, as when he vainly refuses to take "no" for an answer. Upon an adverse decision, interlocutory or final, the proper exception should be taken, or motion entered without the slightest mark of irritation. Petulance under these circumstances is ridiculous, and yet men of reputation and experience often place themselves in an undignified position upon occasions of unfavorable forensic fortune.

§ 145. *Argument before the Court.*— In arguing a case before the court it is, of course, necessary that you should observe order and proper arrangement, state your point distinctly, and sustain each position taken with authorities. Of course, if you can, your cases should be directly in point, or as near it as may be. Cases, so indirectly bearing upon the point at issue as to require a long argument to show that they are applicable at all, are of little value. However learned the judge may be, it is best not to presume too much upon his memory. Except in the simplest propositions, cite the authorities even if you do not read them. A

multiplicity of authorities is injudicious; for to say nothing
of wearying the court and yourself, the appearance of ped-
antry is objectionable, and some of the cases may suggest
distinctions and differences adverse to your views, which
had previously escaped the attention of your learned friend
on the other side. In this, as in other matters, do no works
of supererogation; cite all necessary authorities as strong
as you can get them, and no more. If you have supplementary authorities, it is well enough to reserve them for
your reply.

It is superfluous to say that a very strict attention should
be paid to the instructions given by the court to the jury,
and in asking instructions in favor of your views, be sure
and make your statement of the point as clear as possible.
The court will not be confused by your ambiguity, but the
jury may; for they will take your point from your own
statement, and not from that of the court. You will, of
course, take care that every instruction in your favor shall
be clearly given; for however pains-taking and accurate the
judge may be, he will not probably, of his own motion,
instruct as fully as the counsel will think necessary for a
proper understanding of the case by the jury.

CHAPTER XIII.—Gentlemen of the Jury.

§ 146. *Independence of Juries.*— An independent man is a man who cannot be depended upon. An independent jury multiplies the uncertainty by twelve. The institution, although one of the greatest safeguards of English and American liberty, often fails in the rendition of exact justice. Its chief defect is indissolubly connected with its greatest merit. Its uncertainty is the direct consequence of its independence. The latter is the jewel which has been prized a thousand years; the former is its foil, which has always been tolerated as its inseparable adjunct. It is undeniable that a learned and well-trained judge less frequently errs in deciding questions of fact, than do even the most intelligent dozen good and lawful men that ever were impaneled; but it would be a great mistake, nevertheless, to substitute *irrevocably* the permanent and professional for the occasional arbiter. In ordinary times the change would work no mischief, but at every period of disorder and commotion the independence of the jury of one's peers becomes an invaluable security for life, liberty and property.

In considering the merits and defects of the system in its every-day operation, the first and most striking point in its favor is that juries are unstained by corruption, and that whatever else may cause a failure of justice at their hands, it is never their personal and individual interests. They are excerpts from the mass of the people, and, unless selected in some very defective manner, fairly represent the average honesty and intelligence of the community. When they fail to do justice, it is because of the want of adaptation of their faculties to the abnormal exercises sometimes required of them, or of prepossessions already existing in their minds, or the effect of the address or dexterity of counsel. Practically, this evil is neutralized by the advisory instructions of the bench and the facilities for new trials afforded by the law. With all its faults, however, the institution as it exists in England and America is the best and safest means ever yet devised by the wit of man to ascertain the truth, in matters of fact, for judicial purposes.

§ 147. *Peremptory Challenges.*— In civil cases the advocate has usually, in practice, little part in the selection of juries, though there are provisions for special juries in some of the States, and should be everywhere. In the graver criminal cases, however, the defendant has a negative voice in the selection of the arbiters of his destiny. It therefore becomes a very grave question, involving a heavy responsibility, how the counsel can exercise the right of peremptory challenge to the greatest advantage of his client. You should cautiously husband this prerogative. Take care that you have the jury-list in good time, study it, and challenge " for cause," whenever your information indicates that by that means you can get rid of an obnoxious juror. Thus you have an additional peremptory challenge to expend upon the remainder of the *venire* or the talesmen. Object to all men whom you have reason to believe subject to strong adverse influences in relation to the offense on trial. If, in a murder case, there is presented as a juror a man whose son or brother has been killed, even long ago, and the homicide escaped punishment — have none of him. Naturally, he is unconsciously prejudiced. In a trial for arson, reject one who has ever suffered loss from incendiary fires. And so with all similar cases. As a general rule, challenge all nota-

bly hard-headed, obstinate men ; for they are bundles of
prejudices, and incapable of evolving an impartial opinion.
Men of this stamp are too ready to assume responsibility,
and are not amenable to the appeals for caution and deliberate action which are often effectual with those of less
self-sufficient temperament. When a man of good character has so far fallen under suspicion that a true bill has been
found against him, and he has actually been arraigned, you
may be sure that if he is innocent, there have been very foul
practices on the part of the prosecution, or else an extraordinary combination of adverse circumstances ; and in such
a case you will need a jury not only fair, but highly intelligent and respectable. Such a jury can, with your assistance,
unravel the mysteries of the case, and will acquit your client if
he is innocent, but will certainly convict him if he is guilty—
for the solid man of business, *pater-familias*, church-mem-
ber, of correct habits, is apt to be a just and stern juror,
and has a vivid sense of what is due to the interests of society, and a perfect willingness to promote them by a strict
discharge of his duty. In all questions in which character
is involved, the jurors should be selected from men of *genuine respectability*, for these fine issues are not likely to be
fully appreciated by those less worthily endowed.

§ 148. *Direct, Plain, Simple.* — Juries most readily accept the direct and obvious solution of the problems submitted to them, that which requires only a few simple
deductions and inferences to arrive at a conclusion. They
will not elaborate additional elements of decision, or follow
a complicated line of argument to its logical result. They
are intolerant of explanations and qualifications, and the
advocate whose safety lies in explaining away simple and
stubborn facts has an arduous task before him. A politician many years ago had an ugly record (politically speaking) on the Annexation of Texas question. He was a
candidate for office and was beaten. A political friend ac-
counted for his defeat thus : " The whole of his speeches
was required to explain his course on the Texas question —

and then it was as clear as mud." The people will not submit to a long string of explanations from the politician. The jury, which is an epitome of the people, requires in like manner of the advocate a plain, simple, direct case, clearly stated and fairly argued. In those words "simple," " direct," " plain," is to be found the key to most verdicts. In their ordinary avocations jurymen are accustomed to deal only with simple propositions, and when it becomes necessary to investigate a complicated transaction, they approach it with repugnance, and will look with favor upon almost any hypothesis which involves a simple solution. In the human body are muscles which are habitually unused, and when occasion brings them into play, the exercise is painful and laborious. The juryman's mental muscles, so to speak, are, for want of habitual use, inadequate to the task of solving complicated and involved questions. The mental muscles of the advocate, on the contrary, are thoroughly trained to that special end ; it is his duty to analyze, sift, simplify and present to the jury the facts of the case. divested, as far as possible, of all complexity—in such a shape, indeed, that they become amenable to the common sense which is always held to be the special faculty of the jury.

§ 149. *How to Address a Jury.*— In addressing a jury, an advocate's manner should be plain, straightforward, and, above all things, natural. Make no effort at fine effects ; for appropriate gesticulation is unconsciously suggested by the words as they are spoken ; and felicitous illustration, flashes of eloquence, emanate naturally from the mind surcharged with the electricity of the subject. Strive to present your case, clothed in apt words, in such a manner as will keep up *continuous* interest in the juror. It is not absolutely essential that your speech be wise or even witty—of course, within reasonable limits, the wiser and the wittier, the better—but it must address itself to the juror, enlist his sympathies, gently exercise his intelligence, and titillate his imagination. If too deep and technical for him, he revolts at once ; if too shallow and frivolous—if you give too loose a rein to your wit, or mistake for that admirable but dangerous and very indefinite quality, mere animal spirits and hilarious antics, you lose your hold, and fall a victim to your indiscretion. Indulge in no digression, unless you are quite sure that you are escorted on your excursion by the whole panel. Steadfastly deny yourself all exercise upon your individual hobbies, and all displays of personal or special erudition, which may even possibly prove " caviare to the general," and by all means, at all hazards, at any sacrifice, you must *never, never*, be dull. If the thread of interest is once broken, it is nevermore to be restored, *hiatus valde deflendus* — a solution of continuity past all surgery. Rather than risk this catastrophe, an advocate should sacrifice all personal considerations, individual idiosyncracies, hobbies, crotchets and caprices — everything, in short, save truth and duty, to his stern determination to be heard and to win his case.

Cultivate a lucid, succinct, vigorous style ; eschew involutions ; for although we have the witty rejoinder of William Evarts that " the only people who ought to object to long sentences are the criminals who deserve them," still verbal complications do not commend themselves to the jury.

§ 150. *Inequitable Demands or Defenses.*—All jurors are averse to captious, inequitable or purely technical positions, and when a case stands solely on such grounds, they yield a verdict only to positive and peremptory instructions from the bench. Whenever, therefore, that kind of argument can safely be sent to the rear, and more meritorious grounds relied on, it is best to do so. Where a fairly good case, for example, is supplemented by the statute of limitations, or a plea of usury, do not obtrude these obnoxious and unpopular defenses ; do not abandon them altogether, of course, but press the more morally equitable positions, and let that of prescription or usury take a merely auxiliary and secondary place, and be in effect brought forward in the instructions of the court.

(12)

§ 151. *Feeling.*—In endeavoring to enlist the indignation
or the compassion of the jury, an advocate should make sure
that he has a sound substratum of fact upon which to build
his superstructure of feeling.   Juries are, in these matters,
not unlike the average Englishman as described by Sydney
Smith.   In appealing to him in a case of distress for a
charity, you may vainly ply your most ardent appeals to his
benevolence, and portray the distress and suffering of the
proposed objects of his bounty in the most heart-rending
style.   You effect nothing.   He is methodical and accurate; he requires the day of the month and the year of
the Lord, the certificate of the parson of the parish and the
attestation of two substantial householders.   When he has
these affecting facts, John Bull can hold out no longer; he
yields, he blubbers, he subscribes.

§ 152. *Appeal to Sense of Duty.* — Impress the jury
with an appreciation of your earnestness.   They will re-
spond with a like feeling, and this is highly desirable
in view of the necessity of imbuing them with a realiza-
tion of their responsibility and the importance of their
functions.   In this matter of earnestness, the spurious is
readily detected.   If you do not feel what you are saying,
the fact will become apparent — it will be divined, if not
seen;

> "Pleads he in earnest?   Look upon his face—
> His eyes do drop no tears, his prayers are in jest."

An earnest appeal to the sense of duty and obligation is
effective even with men who would not readily be suspected
of delicate susceptibilities; for conscience, however dwarfed
and dormant, is inherent in human nature.   Avail yourself
of this, and strive to impress the jury with a due regard for
the gravity, and, in extreme cases, the solemnity of the crisis,
and especially with an appreciation of their duty and great
responsibility.

CHAPTER XIV.—ILLUSTRATIVE CASES.

§ 153. THE POSTMAN'S CASE.

A postman was indicted for stealing a shilling. A second indictment charged him with obtaining it by false pretenses with intent to defraud. This was the charge upon which he was tried.

EVIDENCE: He received as a letter-carrier, on the 10th of April, from the post-office a letter to deliver on his ordinary round. It was directed "Miss Brown, No. 50, Grayham Street." The letter was a soldier's letter from Zululand, and was entitled to come post free. The prisoner inquired of a Mrs. Smith where Miss Brown lived, as she had removed from No. 50. Mrs. Smith would show him. The prisoner said "there is a shilling to pay." Some one, but not the post-office authorities, had marked the letter 1 s. in pencil; evidence tended to prove prisoner had marked it himself.

Mrs. Smith took the prisoner to a Mrs. Jones, and said that was where Miss Brown had removed to. On arriving, Mrs. Smith said to Mrs. Jones, " here is a letter for Miss Brown, and there is a shilling to pay," whereupon the prisoner handed in the letter, and received the shilling; Mrs. Jones remarking that Miss Brown would be only too glad to pay the shilling, for " the letter was one she was expecting from her brother from the wars." Mrs. Smith said jocularly, " let us spend the shilling." " No," answered the conscientious postman, " it does not belong to me, I have got to pay it in." Both these witnesses knew the prisoner; and the would-be spendthrift, Smith, knew him well, as would seem from her familiarity.

A day or two after, the prisoner was on his round, and again saw the witnesses, whom one might not irreverently call the "merry wives," and Miss Brown. Mrs. Smith said, " this is the postman who brought that letter from Zululand." " Yes," answered the prisoner, "and if it hadn't been for me, she would never have had it at all, for it had been kicking about for several days." The prisoner was identified by several witnesses, by a whole population one might say.   It was a government prosecution.

Two months after, in consequence of Miss Brown reporting to the post-office authorities the circumstances above stated, a letter was addressed by them to the prisoner, calling his attention to the facts, and asking for an explanation.   The prisoner replied (and his letter was in evidence), that, undoubtedly, he must have been on that district at the time, and on the particular delivery when the letter was given out, but he had no recollection of it at all, and certainly *never received the shilling;* he gave the lie direct to that, and that was the awkward point in the case.   The post-office sheets were produced to prove the non-payment over by the prisoner.

This was the case for the prosecution, except the witnesses to identify; and certainly, on paper, it does look a somewhat hopeless one to defend.

The counsel for the defense commenced cross-examining as to identity; the prosecution having taken so much trouble, and called so many witnesses to prove it, it was worth disputing, as you will see.   It was made the chief point on behalf of the crown.   If they established that, all other defenses must be hopeless — so they established it.

It was very curious that the point, fixed upon by the prosecution as their strength, was thought by them the wrong point to attack on the part of the defense.   But it was cross-examined, so far as one or two witnesses were concerned, and then dropped.

The points elicited in cross-examination were these :—

1. The letter had been given out by the post-office authorities on the morning in question without being stamped.   This was an *oversight* on their part.

2. There was another oversight on the part of the authorities at another post-office with regard to the same letter.

3. There was nothing to show that it was a soldier's letter, and entitled to come free.

4. The prisoner might, under the circumstances, have thought a shilling was due upon it, which would be the postage from Zululand.

5. If he had charged a shilling, and then paid it over, it would, although irregular, have been the right and proper thing to do.

6. The sheet for the 11th of April was not produced, and although the shilling did not appear on the pay-sheet of the 10th, the witness would not absolutely swear it was never paid in.

(Probabilities, however, strong the other way, inasmuch as the prisoner said *he never had it.*)

7. The post-office was sometimes guilty of oversights, and the entering the shilling might have been one.

8. The prisoner might by an oversight have omitted to pay it over.

9. His attention was not called to the circumstance till two months after.

10. Multitudes of letters, some requiring payment, others not, had passed through his hands since that time.

11. His frank avowal that he must have received the letter, but did not remember the circumstances.

The learned counsel for the prosecution was, perhaps, justified in thinking, from the apparently *main line* of cross-examination, that identity was the only defense, and he accordingly made it the principal subject of comment in his summing-up. It was, however, stated on behalf of the prisoner, that there was no question as to identity, as he himself had *admitted it in his own handwriting*. The real question was, whether the prisoner, who bore the most excellent character, and had been in the service of the post-office for ten years, had received the shilling *with intent to defraud*, or whether he had received it and then had forgotten to pay it over, and forgotten indeed all about it; or whether he may not even have paid it over, and its entry be on some other sheet. It was not probable that a young man with so valuable a character would sell it for a shilling.

Witnesses to the young man's goodness were called, and the jury without hesitation acquitted. Without saying that the counsel for the prosecution were wrong in the line they took, it is just within the range of possibility that if the cross-examination had not been to identify at all, that matter would have been taken as proved in the summing-up. The eloquence would have been expended on those minor incidents and trifling theories which looked so insignificant while they were being blown about by a breezy cross-examination, but which took root at last, nevertheless, and grew to be such great probabilities under the ripening influence of a warm and genial speech. And then character lit them all up with such pleasant sunshine, that the jury could never look on the dungeon shadows again — and so acquitted.

§ 154. THE POLICEMAN'S CASE.

The next case was that of a policeman who was indicted for stealing the sum of nine shillings and tenpence halfpenny. The facts deposed to by the witnesses were as follows:—In company with a sergeant of the —— Regiment, he had arrested a deserter, and after delivering him up to the authorities, went into a public-house, and called for two glasses of ale. On being served, he paid three penny pieces to the landlady. At this time a man, whom I will name Lounger, was standing with his elbow leaning on the counter, and almost facing the prisoner and the sergeant. He also had some ale before him. While these persons were in front of the bar, a woman came in, called for a glass of ale, and placed on the counter a half-sovereign. The landlady took the coin into a parlor behind the bar for the purpose of getting change. Meanwhile the woman took her ale, and went into the room on the opposite side of the bar. After a minute or so had elapsed, the landlady returned with the change (the sum in question), consisting of silver and copper, and placed it on the counter between the policeman and sergeant, where it lay for about

five minutes.   The landlady, who was a respectable woman, and unimpeachable as to character, swore that after the lapse of that time she saw
the policeman take up the change and put it in his pocket.   She made
no remark as he did so, because she had forgotten whose change it was.
The policeman and the sergeant then quickly finished their ale, and went
away.   In about a minute or so, the woman to whom it belonged came
to the counter, and asked for her money.   Upon that, the landlady, immediately calling to mind the circumstances, exclaimed: " Why, the
policeman has got it! "   Lounger, then aroused in the liveliness of the
situation, said: "Yes he has; I saw him take it."

Upon this they all went to the door, and the sergeant, who lived in the
barracks nearly opposite, was not in sight; but the policeman was seen
going along some hundred yards from the house.   Lounger was then
told by the landlady to go and bring him back.

Instead of Lounger going to the police-constable, it appeared that he
went to the sergeant.   And the landlady, before the magistrates, had
said no more than that she had sent him to the prisoner, but did not see
him again till nearly nine o'clock at night.   (This point should be
borne in mind.)   Lounger's evidence, in addition to the evidence that
he saw the money taken, was that he went to the sergeant and then returned to the public-house and afterwards went after the prisoner, whom
he saw at the police station; that he gave information against him, upon
which he was taken into custody.   The sergeant was called and said
that he saw the money lying on the counter a minute before he and the
prisoner left the house.   *He could not say if it was there when they left.*

This was the case for the prosecution. Upon this evidence it looks
somewhat hopeless.   If either of the two witnesses, the landlady or
Lounger, could be believed, there was no answer to be made.

There were no witnesses to fact for the prisoner.   The defense therefore must rest upon the cross-examination and the improbability of the
story being true, arising mainly from the good character of the person
charged.

I will now state the points made in cross-examination, and the reader
will do well to remember the exact facts narrated above, as given in the
evidence in-chief.

1st. The woman who had given the half sovereign was cross-examined:

Q. " Who was in the bar when you went in? " A. " No one, I believe."
Q. " You placed the half-sovereign on the counter? "   A. " I did."
This was the whole of her evidence.

2nd. The next witness cross-examined was the landlady,

Q. " How long is the counter? "   A. " Five feet."
Q. " Who came into the house first? "   A. " Lounger."
Q. " Who next? "   A. " The two men."
Q. " And then? "   A. " The woman."
Q. " Did the men come to the counter as soon as they came in? "   A.
" Yes."

The Witness: "The woman may not have seen the men when she came in."

Q. "Why do you say that?" No answer.

Q. "Do you know what the last witness has sworn?" A. "She may not have seen them."

This observation on the part of the witness doubtless arose from the fact that she had talked the matter over and knew she was contradicted upon the depositions. It was of course not pursued on behalf of the prisoner. It was a point made, and being taken in connection with the want of memory of the prosecutrix, as to whom the change be onged, was not without value.

Q. "Were there glasses on the counter, between you and the prisoner?" A. "There were."

Q. "And the handles of the beer-engine?" A. "Yes."

Q. "Six of them?" A. "Yes."

Q. "They would reach two-thirds of the way along the middle of the counter?" A. "Yes."

Q. "Did you leave the bar after the prisoner and the sergeant were gone?" A. "I did."

Q. "Who was left?" A. "Lounger."

Q. "And no one else?" A. "No one."

Q. "Were you busy serving other customers in other parts of the house, while the money was on the counter?" A. "I was."

Here I should pause a moment, to call the reader's attention to a somewhat common blunder which might have been made by a very inexperienced counsel. The temptation to ask the following question would have been very great to beginners:

"*Might not some one else have taken it?*"

The answer would have been "No!" to a certainty, with much emphasis. This was matter of argument for the jury, and unless you cut the ground away from you by putting such a question, there would arise in their minds a strong inference that it might be so.

The next question was:

Q. "Did you send Lounger after the prisoner?" A. "I sent him to the sergeant."

Q. "Is that the same as you deposed before the magistrate?" A. "It is."

Depositions produced; found to be *not* the same. It was there stated in accordance with last question, which makes something more than a slight discrepancy; the effect made on the jury being not unimportant.

Q. "That is what you swore?" A. "It is; but I sent him to the sergeant, not to the prisoner."

Here is not only a contradiction, but an improbability, as well as an unreasonable piece of conduct, all which the jury notice as becomes them.

Q. "Did you authorize Lounger to give the policeman into custody?" Question put in a tone that makes her afraid of the consequences, so she answers with considerable emphasis and no little indignation: A. " *Certainly* not! "

Q. "Nor to take any proceedings against the man?" A. " I did not!!" with at least two notes of indignation.

Lounger is next cross-examined, and states that he was sent to the sergeant, and not to the prisoner.

Asked what the latter did with the money after he had taken it from the counter, he said:—"How do I know? He might ha' put it in his 'at for what I know."

This was a foolish answer for the prosecution, but I am inclined to think that one or two stupid-looking questions had worked Lounger into giving a stupid answer, as will sometimes happen.

The sergeant was cross-examined simply as follows:

Q. " You have been in the army many years?" A. " Ten."

Q. " And have risen to the position of sergeant?" A. "Yes."

Q. " Were you on duty on this day with the prisoner, in apprehending a deserter?" A. " Yes."

Q. " You stood close to him and were talking to him while the change was lying on the counter?" A. " I did."

Q. " Did he touch it?" A. "I never saw him."

Q. " Could he have taken it up without you seeing him?" A. "He could not."

Then came the character of the prisoner, not exhibited sensationally like a dancing creature on a tight-rope with a balance-pole, but in a common-place manner and in every-day costume, arranging as it were the probabilities and the improbabilities; not attempting to captivate the weakness of the jury, but appealing only to their good common sense, which good common sense, after short deliberation, returned a verdict of *not guilty.*

It was said afterwards by the chief authority of the police in the county, that his belief was that Lounger did not go to the policeman in the first instance, as stated in the original depositions, for fear the policeman should apprehend him on the same charge, which perhaps would have been awkward for Lounger. Be that as it may, there was immense importance in this discrepancy between the statements, as it led among other matters to the successful result which followed.

§ 155. THE BOOKBINDER'S CASE.

A highly respected tradesman, whom I will call Marks, was indicted with a man herein named Pincher, for stealing and receiving eighty tablets, which were the *titles* of books to be affixed to the covers, and about twenty books of gold leaf. The prosecutor was in a large way of business in the same trade as Marks, and Pincher was in his employment. The prosecutor's evidence was to this effect:—Ten of the tablets I bought at a certain sale. They have a peculiar mark. I bought all that were in stock. Those produced are some of them. The gold-leaf books (three or four) produced, had a *private mark* made by a pin; it was

made because we were being robbed. Several other tablets were sworn
to as his, because they had been *stamped with a tool which had a particular
flaw in it.* None had ever been sold, and the tool was produced.
Pincher had pleaded guilty to stealing the whole of the articles, and
from information given by him a detective went to Marks' house.
Upon a board at the prosecutor's house he had found the words of a
label in gold leaf, which the *prisoner, Marks, was using for the completion
of an order.* On the detective going into the prisoner's house, he said:
" I have come to see some books which you are binding and lettering
for the A. B. C. Board." "What books?" exclaimed Marks; "I have
no books." The detective then said, " As you have given me that answer, I shall search your house," and thereupon proceeded to do so.
At this time a person came in to see Marks, and the latter invited ·him
to go and have a glass of ale. The detective went with them, and they
all returned together. " Then," said the detective, " I saw Marks give
his son a *peculiar look;* I told him so, and said I should now examine
everything in the house." He found a great number of lettered tablets,
among them *those produced,* and sworn to by the prosecutor as having
been *stamped with the tool which contained the flaw.* On these being
found, Marks said, "Oh, I have had them *four or five years.*" It was
proved that the tool had only had the flaw in it for five or six months.

Found also were other tablets, containing *the particular mark,* and
sworn as having been purchased by the prosecutor. On going into a
room in the basement, the detective's attention was attracted to the fact
of something burning, and on removing a kind of tray which had been
placed against the stove, a *number of gold-leaf books* were found burning;
gold was also scattered on the floor. "What is this?" inquired the
detective. "Oh, we are going to tea," said one of the women. "Do
you have gold-leaf tea?" asked the facetious officer; "if you do, it
must come expensive." He then drew out from the fire *three or four
books, with the private mark of the prosecutor on them,* as described. Marks
was then taken into custody.

This was the evidence for the prosecution; chain of circumstances
very strong, if it will only bear the strain of cross-examination.

First, the prosecutor to the following effect in cross-examination:—
Pincher worked for me at binding and lettering. He was in the habit
of using the tool with the flaw in it. He had no right to work in his
leisure for anyone else; I should have discharged him if I had known
it. But if Pincher, being a skilful workman, had worked for anyone
else, he *might have taken the tool with the flaw in it, and used it on some
one else's tablets.* This was, of course, self-evident, but worth empha-
sizing by the mouth of the prosecutor.

That was one point, therefore, tolerably well disposed of, if the jury
could be got to take that view, which the character of the accused will
undoubtedly persuade them to do, provided always we can dispose of
the other awkward-looking facts of the case, especially the gold-leaf
tea. The next question was with regard to the tablets marked with a

particular mark (consisting of *another flaw in one of the golden lines*, caused by another defective tool). These, as stated, were bought at a sale—at a Mr. Meredith's sale. But on cross-examination it turned out, that Mr. Meredith having become bankrupt, there was a great sale of the stock-in-trade, which all respectable bookbinders could attend, the defendant among the rest; and as for the prosecutor saying that he bought *all* the tablets in stock on that occasion, that did not seem to satisfy the counsel for the defense, who implied by certain questions that some other goods of like character and quality, and with the self-same flaw in them, might have been on hand *before the sale by auction*, of which Mr. Marks might have purchased some. The prosecutor himself could not deny that there was the possibility of this being the case, and the jury seemed to think there was *probability* as well. As before observed, if possibility, probability perhaps. Another point, therefore, immensely in favor of the prisoner. Still, there was that gold-leaf tea yet to dispose of. *The books with the private mark on them, and on the fire!* How can you get over that? Let us see. Was the defendant or his son in the room at the time of the burning?—The detective says No.

Had Marks ever been out of the detective's custody? No.

Clearly then, *he* had not burnt, nor given any directions to burn, these old books.

Had any word been mentioned up to that moment about books of leaf gold? No.

Had there been any search for such books? There had not.

This question must have been based on knowledge of the fact, or it would have been dangerous. It is not necessary to point out why. The answer was important, as it shows two things clearly enough — first, it was not in consequence of any inquiry for such books that a sudden alarm was raised, lest they should be found; if it had been, guilty knowledge would have been manifest enough; secondly, the thief, who had given information, could not have told the detective that he had stolen any books of gold-leaf.

Those two points then are well established. No confession of stealing and no fear of the detective finding any stolen books. Still the private mark *and* the burning. If the mark stood alone, it would conclusively prove that the books were or had been the property of the prosecutor. Does not the burning show guilty knowledge? Not if the defendant did not authorize the burning. The private mark then stands, as I take it, thus: If it can be shown that the books may have come into the house of defendant *without his knowledge*, he is clearly entitled to be acquitted on all points. To show this, it was opened and proved by unimpeachable testimony, that however wrong it might be, Pincher, being an adept at labeling with gold leaf, was employed in the evening by the defendant to letter for him; further, that Pincher always brought his own tools, and *among them the tool in question with the flaw in it*. It was proved that defendant, when his workmen wanted gold-leaf, would give them money to buy it, and that sometimes they would fetch it and **be** paid after; that Pincher was left to work late at night and was given mouey, as others were, to get leaf if required. What more was wanted than this common-sense argument, that Pincher, although having been provided with money to get the leaf with, *stole the books from his master,* instead of purchasing at the proper place and paying for them? If this were so, there would be no guilty knowledge on the defendant's part.

There remains then the burning to get over; for although it is fully explained, that neither the defendant nor his son was present or could have given instructions at the time, it is an awkward and suspicious fact and must be answered somehow.

The jury would like, above all things, to have that point explained, if explained it can be. About which they do not yet despair, seeing how guilty at one time the other two points looked. They know now that innocence itself in the hands of an active and intelligent officer may be so dressed up, as to look like a very Gay Faux of iniquity. There is no explaining the " gold-leaf tea " without witnesses, so the best witnesses are called, namely:— The workmen who *made the fire* with the books. These, examined apart, agree on three important points. That they had *no orders or intimations* of any kind to throw those old books on the fire. That, it being tea time, *they had to light a fire* to boil the kettle. That the detective, in great detective earnestness and activity, rummaged about everywhere, if haply he might find materials to work up into a case, and in so rummaging looked upon a nest of shelves, where old papers and rubbish were, *just over the stove,* and knocked down a small quantity of the said rubbish, among it the valueless old gold-leaf books in question. This was caught up by one of the women and thrown on to the fire, hence the blaze! " Behold, how great a matter a little fire kindleth! " Truly, it was nigh making a very hell of this man's life, that small fire behind the teaboard.

§ 155. A REMARKABLE ESCAPE.

Some years ago a junior was engaged for the prosecution in a case of murder, and he certainly should have been presented by the Royal Humane Society with the medal which it awards to those who have been instrumental in saving life. Whether their gift applies to cases of hanging, as well as drowning, I do not know.

The prisoner had committed a very atrocious murder (I think it was of his wife), and the main evidence against him was the "*dying declaration*" of his victim. Made in his absence, it could only be given in evidence after proof that it was made " with full consciousness of approaching death."

The medical man who attended her was called to prepare the way for the piece of evidence which, if given, would undoubtedly have hanged the prisoner. The humane junior asked—

" Did she *fear* death?" " No," said the doctor. Life-saving junior looked at his attorney, then at his brief, then at the witness.

The witness was perfectly cool, as most doctors are in the witness-box and knew well enough what answer was required. There was not a motion, however, of assistance.

The ingenious young counsel, however, *repeated* the question. "Did she *fear* death?"—Answer: " O, dear no, not at all!" The judge: "You can not put in the statement; that will do, doctor." And you can not find a verdict of guilty, gentlemen, it must be manslaughter! Manslaughter accordingly!

An instructive lesson this to all juniors, to ask the right question; and an excellent lesson to all juniors then present (and to come, now it's published) NOT to cross-examine upon all occasions. One little question put by the counsel for the defense *would have hanged the prisoner;* properly, no doubt (I am not writing in the humane vein), but it was not the *duty* of the counsel who defended the wretch to hang him.

This occurred almost as soon as I was called to the bar, and the scene is as fresh to my mind at this moment as it was then. The blank look on the face of the counsel; the sagacious smile of the judge, who evidently thought the right question would be put next; the quick perceptive glance of the witness, who stood leaning on the witness-box with his hands carelessly folded, and who had just the expression of face which an intelligent being has who asks you to guess something, and finds you answer very near and yet a very long way off—all this is still before me. And I have a vivid sense of the excitement I experienced, as I wondered whether the right question would be put or not. I am sorry to confess to a feeling of disappointment when it was not; for according to my judgment, if ever a man deserved the full benefit of a dying declaration, it was the devil-man in the dock, who escaped only through the blunder of an inexperienced advocate.

The answer of the doctor was undoubtedly both true and untrue. In the letter it was true, in the *meaning* of the question it was untrue; because the woman was unquestionably *conscious of her approaching dissolution*. In a case, however, where life and death hang upon a word, it seems to me the doctor was right in answering according to the letter. Let us at least be accurate and precise in our language, where life or death depend upon it.

APPENDIX.

I.—Whately on Cross-Examination.

In his "Elements of Rhetoric" Archbishop Whately has attempted to cast discredit on the great body of a profession which is as jealous of its high reputation for courtesy and honor, as it is deserving of it. At page 165 he says:

"In oral examination of witnesses, a skilful cross-examiner will often elicit from a reluctant witness most important truths which the witness is desirous of concealing or disguising. There is another kind of skill, which consists in so alarming, misleading or bewildering an honest witness as to throw discredit on his testimony, or pervert the effect of it. Of this kind of art, which may be characterized as the most, or one of the most, base and depraved of all possible employments of intellectual power, I shall only make one further observation."

I pause here for a moment to say that, so far as my experience of the bar is concerned, and I think it must be greater than that of the Right Reverend Father in God who penned these words, a more undeserved slander against a body of honorable men was never penned even by a churchman. He proceeds to say:

"I am convinced that the most effectual mode of eliciting truth is quite different from that by which an honest, simple-minded witness is most easily baffled and confused. I have seen the experiment tried of subjecting a witness to such a kind of cross-examination by a practised lawyer, as would have been, I am convinced, the most likely to alarm and perplex many an honest witness without any effect in shaking his testimony."

According to the archbishop's views, the course the most likely to alarm and perplex an honest witness has no effect upon the dishonest one. This falls in with my own experience so far, but I think it is impossible to "shake" an honest witness' testimony except by the means I have endeavored to indicate. But we have only the archbishop's word for the "practised lawyer." He then proceeds:

"And afterwards, by a totally opposite mode of examination, such as would not have at all perplexed one who was honestly telling the truth" (nothing it seems will perplex an honest witness but an alarming style)—"that same witness was drawn on, step by step, to acknowledge the utter falsity of the whole,

Generally speaking, I believe that a quiet, gentle and straightforward—though full and careful—examination, will be the most adapted to elicit truth, and that the manœuvres and the browbeating which are the most adapted to confuse an honest witness, are just what the dishonest one is best prepared for."

When I read those wordy sentences, I could not help thinking it was a pity that the archbishop did not confine himself to theology. He seems to think an honest witness easily baffled and frightened into telling a lie, and to imagine that a brutal liar is best induced to tell the truth by wooing him with sweet words, and by a straightforward, full and careful examination.

II. — CROSS-EXAMINATION OF A MEDICAL WITNESS.

The following, taken from the Palmer case, is regarded as a very fine specimen of the cross-examination of a medical witness:

Q. "To what constitutional symptoms about Cook do you ascribe the convulsions from which he died?" A. "Not to any."

Q. "Was not the fact of his having syphilis an important ingredient in your judgment upon the case?"—A. "It was. I judge that he died from convulsions, by the combination of symptoms."

Q. "What evidence have you to lead you to suppose that he was liable to excitement and depression of spirits?"—A. "The fact that after winning the race he could not speak for three minutes."

Q. "Anything else?"—"A. "Mr. Jones stated that he was subject to mental depression. Excitement will produce a state of brain which will be followed at some distance by convulsions. I think Dr. Bamford made a mistake when he said the brain was perfectly healthy."

Q. "Do you mean to set up that opinion against that of Dr. Devonshire and Dr. Harland who were present at the *post mortem?*"—A. "My opinion is founded in part on the evidence taken at the inquest, in part on the depositions. With the brain and the system in the condition in which Cook's were, I believe it is quite possible for convulsions to come on and destroy a person. I do not believe that he died from apoplexy. He was under the influence of morphia. I can't ascribe his death to morphia, except that it might assist in producing a convulsive attack. I should consider morphia not very good treatment, considering the state of excitement he was in. Morphia, when given in an injured state of the brain, often disagrees with the patient."

Q. "But what evidence have you as to the injured state of the brain?"—A. "Sickness often indicates it. I can't say whether the attack on Sunday night was an attack of convulsions. I think that the Sunday attack was one of a similar character, but not so intense as the attack of Tuesday, in which he died. I don't think he had convulsions on the Sunday, but he was in that condition which often precedes convulsions."

Q. "Have you ever known a case of convulsions of a tetanic form from intestinal irritation terminating in death, in which the patient remained conscious to the last?"—A. "I have not. Where epilepsy terminates in death, consciousness is gone."

Q. "Can you tell me of any case of death from convulsions, in which the patient was conscious to the last?"—A. "I do not know of any. Convulsions, occurring after poison has been taken, are properly called tetanic."

The *Attorney-General:* "We are told by Sir Benjamin Brodie that while the paroxysms of tetanic convulsion last, there is no difference between those which arise from strychnine and those which arise from tetanus, properly so-called, but the difference was in the course the symptoms took. Now, what do you say is the difference between tetanus arising from strychnine and ordinary tetanus?'

A. "The hands are less violently contracted; the effect of the spasm is less in ordinary tetanus. The convulsion, too, never entirely passes away. I have stated that tetanus is a disease of days, strychnine of hours and minutes; that convulsive twitchings are in strychnine the first symptoms, the last in tetanus; that in tetanus the hands, feet and legs are usually the last affected, while in strychnine they are the first. I never said that Cook's case was that of idiopathic tetanus. I do not think it was a case of tetanus in any sense of the word It differed from the course of tetanus from strychnine in the particulars I have already mentioned."

The *Attorney- General:* "Repeat them."—A. "There was the sudden accession of the convulsions."

· Q. "Sudden—after what?"—A. "After the rousing by Jones. There was also the power of talking."

Q. " Don't you know that Mrs. Smyth talked and retained her consciousness to the end? That her last words were 'turn me over?'" [There was undoubtedly poison by strychnine in the case of Mrs. Smyth.]—A. "She did say something of that kind. I believe that in poison tetanus the symptoms are first observed in the legs and feet. In the animals upon which I have experimented, twitchings in the ears and difficulty of breathing have been the premonitory symptoms."

Q. " When Cook felt a stiffness and difficulty of breathing, and said he should be suffocated on the first night, what were those but premonitory symptoms?" A. "Well, he asked to be rubbed; but as far as my experience goes with regard to animals—"

The *Attorney- General:* "They can't ask to have their ears rubbed, of course" (a laugh).—A. "In no single instance could the animals bear to be touched."

Q. " Did not Mrs. Smyth ask to have her arms and legs rubbed?"—A. "In the Leeds case, the lady asked to be rubbed before the convulsions came on, but afterwards she could not bear it, and begged that she might not be touched."

Q. " Can you point out in any one point, after the premonitory symptoms, in which the symptoms in this case differ from those of strychnine tetanus?"— A. "There is the power of swallowing, which is taken away by inability to move the jaw."

Q. " But have you not stated that lockjaw is the last symptom that occurs in strychnine tetanus?"—A. "I have. I don't deny that it may be. I am speaking of the general rule. In the Leeds case it came on very early, more than two hours before death, the paroxysms having continued about two hours and a half. In that case we believe that the dose was four times repeated. Poison might probably be extracted by-chemical process from the tissues, but I never tried it except in one case of an animal. I am not sure whether poison was in that case given through the mouth. We killed four animals with reference to the Leeds case; and in every instance we found strychnine in the contents of the stomach. In one case we administered it by two processes, and one failed and the other succeeded."

With regard to medical opinion, Sir Alexander Cockburn said: " A medical man ought to be asked his opinion on the supposition only that certain symptoms existed."

III. — MEDICAL CERTAINTY.

An eminent Queen's Counsel told me, *apropos* of the quickness with which medical practitioners sometimes arrive at a conclusion, of a case that occurred some years ago. A woman who had cohabited with a tradesman in a country village, suddenly disappeared. Her paramour gave out that she had gone to America. Some years after, a skeleton was found in the garden of the house where she had lived. On examination by a medical man, he at once pronounced it to be that of the missing woman. He formed this opinion from the circumstance that one of the teeth was gone, and. that he had extracted the corresponding one from the woman some years before. Upon this the prosecution was instituted, and the man was committed for trial to the assizes. Fortunately, there was time, before the trial came on, for a further investigation of the garden where the skeleton was found, and on digging near the spot, another skeleton was discovered, and then another, and another; then several more. This threw some doubt upon the identification of the bones in question, and on further inquiries being made, it turned out that the garden had once been a gipsy burial ground. It need scarcely be added that the prosecution, which had been vigorously taken up by the government, was at once vigorously abandoned.

IV.— INJUDICIOUS CROSS-EXAMINATION.

An example of injudicious cross-examination will illustrate many observations I have made on that subject.

An action was brought against a lessee for non-repair; damages claimed about £300. The witnesses for the plaintiff had shown a want of water-tightness and wind-tightness sufficient to raise the expectations of any young counsel who could restrain his powers of cross-examination. But it is one of the most extraordinary features in advocacy, that few can resist the temptation to evil that lurks in that fascinating privilege. In this case the enterprising counsel for the plaintiff performed an acrobatic feat of cross-examination, and attempting to turn a double somersault alighted on his head.

Witness for the defense had said that the house *was in a fair state of repair:*

Q. " It was in *splendid condition*, wasn't it?" (Imagine, if·you can that *this* is cross-examination).

A. "I did not say it was in *splendid* condition. I said it was in tenantable repair."

Q. " *Then what has been said by the witnesses for the plaintiff is pure imagination?*"

A. "I don't know about pure imagination. I know it is a *got-up-job*." (Laughter).

The witness, like a skilful arguer, limited his answer by appropriate terms.

" I don't mind your saying that," retorted the counsel, " it doesn't hurt me."

He was mistaken; it did hurt him, for the jury believed the last answer of the witness, and gave only trifling damages.

The second question in this cross-examination and its answer *lost the case to the plaintiff.*

V.— ANALYSIS OF THE OPENING SPEECH OF SIR ALEXANDER COCKBURN, IN THE TRIAL OF PALMER FOR THE MURDER OF COOK BY POISON, IN 1856.

One can not help remarking, at the outset, the fine rhetorical simplicity of the exordium:

"Gentlemen of the jury, the duty which you are called upon to discharge is the most solemn which a man can by possibility be called upon to perform; it is to sit in judgment, and to decide an issue on which depends the life of a fellow-creature, who stands charged with the highest crime for which man can be arraigned before a worldly tribunal."

Then follows a detail of Palmer's pecuniary embarrassments, ranging from 1853 to Cook's death. During this period he forged his mother's name to acceptances, and insured his brother's life, and raised money upon the security of the policy. By his wife's death, in 1854, he realized from an insurance on her life £13,500, which retarded his pecuniary ruin. Other bill transactions, however, followed, and finally he forged Cook's name to a check and obtained the money upon it. Then follows an abortive attempt to insure for £25,000 the life of one Bates, a *hanger-on in his stables.*

"All these circumstances," says the Attorney-General, "are important, *because they show the desperate straits in which the prisoner at that time found himself.*"

Then followed letters from a solicitor, Pratt, to Palmer, pressing upon him the necessity of meeting the numerous bills bearing the acceptance of *Sarah Palmer.*

On the 6th of November, Pratt issued two writs for £4,000, one against Palmer, and the other against his mother. The writs, however, were held back for a time, Palmer being constantly pressed by Pratt to raise money. On the 13th of November, Pratt wrote urging Palmer to raise £1,000 to meet the bills due on the 9th.

Then it is stated, that at the Shrewsbury races Cook had won the sum of £2,050.

These are the circumstances which the learned Attorney-General referred to as *not immediately connected with the accusation, but which it would be necessary to look to. They are those out of which the motive arose, and they come first in the order of time.* When he comes to the last transaction referred to, he makes the brief, but pregnant remark, "*Within a week from that time Mr. Cook died.*" Then he says, keeping logically and impressively straight to the main issue, as if that were never to be lost sight of for a single moment, whatever the complication of circumstances through which he must pass: "The important inquiry which we have now to make is, *how he came by his death,* whether by natural causes or by the hand of man, and if the latter, by whose hand?" That was the question.

The Attorney-General then mentions the state of Cook's health, his excitement at having won the race, and proceeds to detail "*a remarkable incident,*" which occurred in the evening of the day after the race in which Cook had been so successful.

Late in the evening Fisher went into a room in which he found Palmer and Cook drinking brandy and water. Cook gave him something to drink, and said to Palmer, "You'll have some more, won't you?" Palmer replied, " Not unless you finish your glass." Cook said, " I'll soon do that, and he finished it at a gulp, leaving only about a teaspoonful at the bottom of the glass. He had hardly swallowed it, when he exclaimed, " Good God! there's something in it; it burns my throat." Palmer immediately took up the glass, and drinking what remained, said : " Nonsense, there's nothing in it," and then pushing the glass to Fisher and another person who had come in, said : " Cook fancies there is something in the brandy and water; there's nothing in it; taste it." On which one of them replied, " How can we taste it? You've drunk it all." Cook suddenly rose, and left the room, and called out, saying that he was taken seriously ill. He was seized with the most violent vomiting, and became so bad, that after a little while it was necessary to take him to bed.

From Shrewsbury, Palmer and Cook went together to Rugeley, and there occurred " an incident connected with the occurrences at Shrewsbury," which has to be mentioned, and that was that " about eleven o'clock that night, a Mrs. Brooks, who betted on commission, and had an establishment of jockeys, went to speak to the deceased on some racing business, and in the lobby she saw Palmer holding up a tumbler to the light, and, having looked at it through the glass, he withdrew to an outer room, and presently returned with the glass in hand and went into the room where Cook was, and in which room he drank the brandy and water, from which, I suppose, you will infer that the sickness came on."

The reader will see that here the order of time is not quite strictly followed, otherwise this incident would have come before the drinking of the liquid; but he will observe the force of this mode of filling in an important circumstance, which, standing utterly by itself, may be taken and fitted into its place at any moment, and certainly attracts more attention by halting in the narrative for the purpose of doing so.

"I do not charge," the Attorney-General continues, "that by anything which caused that sickness Cook's death was occasioned; but I shall show you that throughout the ensuing days at Rugely he constantly received things from the prisoner, and that during those days that sickness was continued. I shall show you that after he died, antimony was found in the tissues of his body and in his blood — antimony administered in the form of tartar-emetic, which, if continued to be applied, will maintain sickness. It was not that, however, of which this man died. *The charge is* that, *having been prepared by antimony, he was killed by strychnine.*"

Now, up to this time, strychnine had not been mentioned, and if the jury had been thinking that antimony was the agent employed to take away Cook's life, they must have been greatly surprised when they were told it was not; and their surprise must have been greater still, and enhanced with the sense of gratified curiosity, when they were told the reason of its having been used, and the real poison which caused the deceased's death. I can not help thinking that this is worthy of study, for its rhetorical effect.

Next comes a description of strychnine, its source, nature, and effects upon animal life; and particularly the fact, that from half to three-quarters of a grain will destroy life. Then a description of the nervous organization of man, upon which this subtle poison exercises its deadly power. Here is manifested a power and skill which the reader can not too carefully study.

He says: "Strychnine affects the nerves which act on the voluntary muscles, and it leaves wholly unaffected the nerves on which human consciousness depends, and it is important to bear this in mind—some poisons produce a total absence of consciousness, but the poison to which I refer affects the voluntary action of the muscles of the body, and leaves unimpaired the power of consciousness."

This was the point in the case, as will appear hereafter; and it was extracted from the mass of circumstances as skilfully as the subtle poison is extracted by the " skill of the operative chemist from the vegetable product known as *nux vomica*."

" Now, the way in which strychnine acting upon the voluntary muscles is fatal to life is, that it produces the most intense excitement of all those muscles, violent convulsions take place—spasms, which affect the whole body, and which end in rigidity; all the muscles become fixed, and the respiratory muscles in which the lungs have play are fixed with an immovable rigidity; respiration consequently is suspended, and death ensues. These symptoms are known to medical men under the term of *tetanus*. There are other forms of *tetanus* which produce death, and which arise from other causes than the taking of strychnine; but there is a wide difference between the various forms of the same disease, which prevents the possibility of mistake."

To prevent that possibility, the learned counsel distinguished between the different forms of *tetanus*, and described their symptoms, one form being known as *traumatic*, and the other as *idiopathic*; one characteristic of *tetanus* from strychnine being that " the paroxysms commence with all their power at the very first, and terminate, after a few short minutes of fearful agony and struggles, in the dissolution of the victim."

This point in the opening speech being arrived at, the reader will have observed that all is now ready for the plain matter-of-fact evidence. Everything is prepared for it. All the branches of fact are placed in order, and converge to a common center; the jury know all about the turf propensities of the prisoner; they know that he had forged his mother's name, and that he was in danger of being convicted of felony; they more than suspect that he took away his brother's life; that he intended to destroy Bates; they have a suspicion that the £13,000 which he obtained from the insurance-office was the price of his wife's life;

they know that Cook was an easy, foolish man, and that the prisoner
was a cunning and rapacious knave; they know that Palmer put the antimony into the brandy-and-water; they know all about the two sets of
nerves, what strychnine is, and how it kills by *tetanus;* they know that
there are three kinds of *tetanus,* and that two sorts always commence with
mild symptoms, gradually increasing, while the *tetanus* produced by
strychnine comes on all at once and.kills very quickly. They can't mistake *traumatic* and *idiopathic* from *tetanus* produced by poison. They will
discern the difference in a moment whe they see the symptoms.

Palmer attended on Cook for days, and during the whole time Cook's
sickness continued. Whatever was sent by Palmer had the same effect.
A woman at the inn, who tasted some broth that had been sent over from
Palmer's house, was taken ill immediately after. On the Saturday a
Dr. Bamford was called in, and Palmer told him that Cook had been
dining too freely, and had a bilious attack. This was false, and unnecessarily false, if Palmer was innocent. And this led the Attorney-
General to the task of proving that it was false, by showing that there
was no bilious symptom whatever during the whole time of Cook's sickness. Coffee, administered while Palmer was present, produced vomiting; barley-water, at six when he was not there, did not have the same
effect; at eight when he was present again, vomiting was once more
produced by arrowroot.

The Attorney-General says: "These may be coincidences, but they are
facts, which, of whatever interpretation they may be susceptible, are well
deserving of attention."

During Cook's illness Palmer went to London, on Monday, and in his
absence Cook's health decidedly improved. While in London, Palmer
conferred with Herring, a man on the turf, whom he engaged to settle
Cook's accounts, not mentioning Fisher, who usually did so. He instructed Herring to collect the sums which Cook was entitled to receive;
and out of the money to pay certain of *his (Palmer's) own debts,* telling
Herring that Cook had had a dose of calomel and must not come out.

In the evening Palmer returned to Rugeley, arriving at about 9 o'clock,
visited Cook, and from 10 till 11 was constantly in and out of Cook's
room. Just at this point, while he is in and out of Cook's room, the
learned counsel informs the jury that "in the course of the evening he
went to a man named Newton, assistant to a man named Salt, and applied
for three grains of strychnine, which Newton, knowing Palmer to be a
medical man, did not hesitate to give him. And," he continued, "Dr.
Bamford had sent on this day the same kind of pills that he had sent on
Saturday and Sunday. I believe it was the doctor's habit to take the
pills himself to the 'Talbot Arms' and entrust them to the care of the
housekeeper, who carried them upstairs; but it was Palmer's practice to
come in afterwards, and evening after evening to administer medicine to
the patient. There is no doubt that Cook took pills on Monday night.
Whether he took the pills prepared for him by Dr. Bamford and similar
to those taken on Saturday and Sunday, or whether Palmer substituted

for Dr. Bamford's pills some of his own construction, consisting in some measure of strychnine, I must leave to the jury to determine."

Then at 12 o'clock at night Cook screams and is taken with convulsions, but he was *conscious*—one of the symptoms, as the jury have got well into their minds, of *tetanus produced by strychnine*. Palmer comes, gives him more medicine, and he vomits. The patient became more calm, and begged the women to rub his limbs. They did so, and found them cold and rigid; (another symptom of *tetanus* produced by strychnine).

Other suspicious circumstances are now detailed, the purchase on Tuesday of strychnine from another shop by Palmer, and an effort made by him to prevent Newton from ascertaining that fact, in which, however, he failed.

Now comes a difficulty, as if for the purpose of showing the student how to deal with it. " And here, I must mention a fact of some importance respecting Mr. Newton. When examined before the coroner, that gentleman only deposed to one purchase of strychnine by Palmer; and it was only as recently as yesterday that, with many expressions of contrition for not having been more explicit, he communicated to the Crown the fact that Palmer had also bought strychnine on Monday night."

The Attorney-General's mode of disposing of this " difficulty " was to place it in his opening speech fairly before the jury, with an intimation that " they must deal with it."

Next follows a statement that Palmer on that day procured one Cheshire to fill up a check in his (Palmer's) favor to be signed by Cook for £350, and said that he would get Cook's signature to it. It is intimated that the signature to that check was forged.

That morning Palmer sent to Cook coffee and broth which produced protracted vomiting, and now a new person makes his appearance on the stage. This new person was a Mr. Jones, a surgeon and personal friend of Cook's. Palmer had written to this gentleman and, foolishly enough, stated that Cook was " suffering from a bilious attack, accompanied with diarrhœa," adding, " it is desirable for you to come to see him as soon as possible." This is considered by the learned counsel " worthy of remark." And the remark is to the effect that the statement was untrue, and probably intended to give color to the idea that Cook died a natural death.

Jones saw at once it was not a bilious attack. At seven o'clock Dr. Bamford called, the patient doing pretty well. Then comes a consultation of the medical men, Palmer, of course, being included, poor Cook exclaiming, " Mind, I'll have no more pills or medicine to-night." He evidently did not believe that they did him any good.

Dr. Bamford made the pills, and Palmer, having asked him to write the directions, carried them off with him, and half or three-quarters of an hour afterward brought the pills to Cook. He called Jones' attention to the handwriting of the direction on the pill-box, observing how distinct and vigorous it was for a man upwards of eighty.

At half-past ten at night the pills are administered, the patient is immediately sick, but the pills are not brought up. At a later period, there is a scream and exclamation from the patient. Palmer is sent for, in two minutes he is beside Cook's bed, saying he had never dressed so quickly in his life. The counsel intimated to the jury that he had not dressed at all; that he was waiting for the catastrophe.

Now then the all-important symptoms are described. Much depends on these being accurately noted, otherwise the *tetanus*, if *tetanus* it be, may be *traumatic* or *idiopathic.* " Cook was found in the same condition, with the same symptoms as the night before; gasping for breath, screaming violently; his body convulsed with cramps and spasms, and his neck rigid. He asked Palmer for the remedy that had relieved him the night before. Palmer goes to fetch it. He comes back with two pills, which he says are ammonia, though the Attorney-General was "assured that it is a drug that requires much time in the preparation, and can with difficulty be made into pills." The pills are taken at once and brought up immediately.

We all know with what dramatic effect a man dies on the stage when a great tragedian has the part. Let us see how a man dies at the hands of a great master of narrative, when the mind has been prepared for the scene and the circumstances: "And now ensued a terrible scene. He was instantly seized with violent convulsions; by degrees his body began to stiffen out; then suffocation commenced. Agonized with pain, he repeatedly entreated to be raised. They tried to raise him, but it was not possible. The body had become rigid as iron, and it could not be done. He then said: 'Pray turn me over.' He gasped for breath, but could utter no more. In a few moments all was tranquil—the tide of life was ebbing fast. Jones leant over him to listen to the action of the heart. Gradually the pulse ceased—all was over—he was dead!"

Now comes the great point, made the central object in this dramatic scene.

"I will show you that this was a death referable in its symptoms to the *tetanus* produced by strychnine, and not to any other possible form of *tetanus.*"

A number of incidents are then enumerated, showing that after Cook's death Palmer had busied himself about the affairs of the deceased, searched the pockets of his coat, that his letters and betting-book were missing, that Palmer tried to induce Cheshire to attest Cook's signature to a paper forty-eight hours after his death. When Stevens, Cook's father-in-law, tells Palmer that he will have a *post-mortem* examination, Palmer offered to nominate the surgeon, and that upon Palmer's importunity Dr. Bamford filled up the customary certificate, and entered the cause of death as apoplexy.

This was a circumstance not in favor of the prosecution, and the learned Attorney-General deals with it on the spot. "Dr. Bamford is upwards of eighty, and I hope that it is to some infirmity connected with his great age, that this most unjustifiable act is to be attributed.

However, he shall be produced in court, and he will tell you that apoplexy has never been known to produce *tetanus*."

In fact, he should be his own antidote. Perhaps that was a better thing to do than to get some one else to contradict his certificate.

Palmer sends for Newton, and singularly enough at this time wants to know how much strychnine will kill a dog, and "how much would be found in the tissues and intestines after death." Awkward questions, certainly, for the defense to deal with. Newton replied none at all: "but that is a point," says the Attorney-General, "on which I will produce important evidence." Palmer tells the medical men who conducted the *post-mortem* that Cook had had epileptic fits; that they would find "old disease in the heart and head;" that the poor fellow was "full of disease," and had all kinds of complaints." All these statements were completely disproved by the *post-mortem* examination. Liver, lungs and kidneys, all healthy. And there was nothing to cause death; not a trace of poison was found, not even at the second examination, after the exhumation of the body sometime afterwards. Palmer was delighted, and turning to Dr. Bamford, exclaimed, "Doctor, they won't hang us yet!"

There were other statements of suspicious conduct at the *post-mortem* examination, and, among other things, an attempt by Palmer to bribe the postboy to upset his vehicle, and break the jar containing the stomach and intestines which were to be subjected to analysis. It is further stated that Palmer sent presents to the coroner, and that prior to the Shrewsbury races he had no money, and afterwards was flush of cash. The following is a summary of the circumstances, showing Palmer's position, and how he was reduced to the desperate extremity of forging acceptances:

"With ruin staring him in the face, you, gentlemen, must say whether he had not sufficient inducement to commit the crime." But there was a further object; "the claim of £4,000 which he said he had against Cook for bills; and he wanted Polestar;" further "the fact, too, that Cook was mixed up in the insurance of Bates, may lead one to surmise that he was in possession of secrets relating to the desperate expedients to which this man had resorted to obtain money. I will leave you to say whether this combination of motives may not have led to the crime with which he is charged. This you will only have to consider, supposing the case to be balanced between probabilities; but if you believe the evidence as to what took place on the Monday and the Tuesday— if you believe the paroxysms of the Monday, the mortal agony of the Tuesday — I shall show that things were administered on both those days by the hand of Palmer, by a degree of evidence almost amounting to certainty."

In conclusion, the Attorney-General stated that although the detection of strychnine in the human body, after death, was a matter of great uncertainty, its effects were distinguishable from those of all other agents, and that, although the analysis failed to yield evidence of the presence of strychnine, it showed the presence of antimony, but for what purpose that drug was administered he admits is uncertain — either, perhaps, to destroy the patient directly, or bring about such appearance of disease as to account for his death.